I0128302

Albert B. Bach

The Art Ballad

Loewe and Schubert, with musical illustrations

Albert B. Bach

The Art Ballad
Loewe and Schubert, with musical illustrations

ISBN/EAN: 9783744795807

Printed in Europe, USA, Canada, Australia, Japan

Cover: Foto ©Thomas Meinert / pixelio.de

More available books at **www.hansebooks.com**

The Art Ballad

LOEWE AND SCHUBERT

WITH MUSICAL ILLUSTRATIONS

BY

ALBERT B. BACH

HONORARY MEMBER OF THE ROYAL ACADEMY OF MUSIC, FLORENCE

AUTHOR OF 'MUSICAL EDUCATION AND VOCAL CULTURE,'
'MOZART, RAPHAEL, AND THE RENAISSANCE,'
'PRINCIPLES OF SINGING,' ETC.

THIRD EDITION

WILLIAM BLACKWOOD AND SONS
EDINBURGH AND LONDON
MDCCCXCI

All Rights reserved

TO

Her Most Gracious Majesty the Queen,

THIS BOOK ON LOEWE

(WHO, WITH GRATITUDE, RECALLED THE HOURS WHEN
HE HAD THE HONOUR OF SINGING HIS BALLADS BEFORE
HER MAJESTY AND THE PRINCE CONSORT, AT WINDSOR)

IS, BY PERMISSION, RESPECTFULLY DEDICATED,

BY HER MAJESTY'S GRATEFUL AND

DEVOTED SERVANT,

ALBERT B. BACH.

CONTENTS.

—

THE ART BALLAD.

JOHANN CARL GOTTFRIED LOEWE.

FRANZ SCHUBERT.

LOEWE'S BALLADS.

PREFACE TO THIRD EDITION.

I cannot but observe with satisfaction the widespread interest which has lately been manifested in the works of Loewe, both in Great Britain and Germany, and it is to this that I attribute the fact of the present work having been translated into German by Dr P. Zunker. It will shortly be published by Robert Lienau (Schlesingersche Buch und Musikhandlung), Berlin. To the same cause I must also attribute the cordial reception which was recently given to my singing of several of Loewe's masterpieces before the Loewe Verein in Berlin, and the fact that I have been invited to take part this season in making the London public better acquainted with Loewe's dramatic Ballads.

Two volumes of Loewe's Ballads with English words, which I have edited and partly translated, were issued last week by R. Lienau of Berlin : these two volumes contain—" Edward," " The Three Wooers," " The Erlking," " Sir Oluf," " Archibald Douglas," " The Fisherman," " The Lost Daughter," " The Clock," " Odin's Ride over the Sea," " The Imprisoned Admiral," " The Monk of Pisa," " Fair Red Rose," " The Nick " (The Water-Sprite).

I hope every vocalist may find something in this collection which will suit his voice and please his taste. " He that bringeth much, will bring something to many."

Fairies, elves, and water-sprites, those interesting beings of an

imaginary world, acquire new life through Loewe's music; and
if the vocalist sings with expression—that is, not only with his
voice, but also with his soul—he will transport us into that ideal
world, and refresh our heart and mind.

ALBERT B. BACH.

EDINBURGH, *May* 1, 1891.

PREFACE TO SECOND EDITION.

AT the Semmering Hotel, near the glorious snow mountain,
the pleasant news reached me that the first edition of the 'Art
Ballad' is out of print, and a second is demanded.   This is a
success which I had scarcely expected, and I am very glad to
have an opportunity of expressing my heartiest thanks to the
press and public for their kind support, and for the interest
which they have demonstrated towards my work.

I have nothing to add nor to alter in the book; I have only
to tell my readers the interesting news that Dr Runze has found
an opera by Loewe, called "Elisabeth"—the libretto is written
after Sir Walter Scott's 'Kenilworth.'   Before I return to Edinburgh, I intend to stay a few days in Berlin, where Dr Runze
will show me the manuscript: perhaps I may be so happy as to
introduce the work to an English audience.

ALBERT B. BACH.

September 5, 1890.

PREFACE.

THE great interest evinced by the public and the press in my illustrated lecture on the "Ballad Airs of Loewe and Schubert," delivered to the members of the Philosophical Institution of Edinburgh, and in my Loewe concert in this city, has resulted in numerous requests that I should issue it in an enlarged form.

I am very glad to have now an opportunity of speaking to the widest audience — the public — on Loewe, the greatest of ballad composers, whose genius paved the way for many other composers, who was a forerunner of Schumann, Mendelssohn, and Wagner, and whose influence we can observe in several of their works and in the works of many modern masters.

B

Loewe deserves special study and appreciation, as he created new forms, not only in the ballad, but also in the oratorio. Without him there would have been a gap in the history of music; and every one who wishes to have a real insight into it must make a thorough study of his works, the knowledge of which is most important if we wish to understand the development of modern music.

That Loewe's ballad airs are not known in Scotland is difficult to understand, as, properly speaking, this is the land of the ballad; and I believe nobody will find it an exaggeration if I say that the literary glory of this country is partly to be attributed to its wonderful ballads.

I am much gratified to see that the ballads of Loewe, although the music was unknown in this country and in spite of the German words, were very favourably received by a Scottish audience; still I am not yet satisfied. As an apostle of Loewe, I shall not cease to work for him, in speaking, singing, and writing; and I hope to see as the result that in future the name of Loewe will more frequently appear in programmes of classical concerts and choral societies, and that great artists will consider it their duty to make the public better acquainted with his sublime works, and win all Scotland for his genius. I believe that hardly any composer has more esteemed and praised Scotland than Loewe has done in his Scottish ballads—"Thomas the Rhymer," "Edward," "The Mother's Ghost," and "Archibald Douglas." Let us therefore give honour to whom honour is due.

I am sorry to observe that there is nothing published in England, either book or pamphlet, on the subject of Loewe; even Sir George Grove's Musical Dictionary devotes only a few lines to the great composer, and that in a very unsatisfactory way. The writer of the article in question was the late Dr F. Gehring, the learned musical critic of the 'Deutsche Zeitung,' with whom I had the pleasure of being acquainted. I find myself unable to agree with his judgment on Loewe, which to me makes it plain that the accomplished critic had, after all, not acquired more than a superficial knowledge of the works of our composer.

It gives me, however, great satisfaction to know that Richard Wagner esteemed very highly even Loewe's first compositions, as he is reported to have said, in reference to the ballad "Edward," "Loewe is a genius!"

There are critics who call Loewe's works old-fashioned, others who find him too eccentric, others again too bold in his harmonies, and so forth.

It must strike the reflective reader how often works of art are superficially criticised and discussed. Where a new chord or a striking dissonance occurs, as, for example, in the "Moorish Prince" or "Edward," and elsewhere, there the theorist appears, and rules that it belongs to the domain of the ugly and the forbidden; but genius discovers and reveals new beauties, and shapes the laws of beauty, and if the fine faculty of the composer finds pleasure in the novel combination, the disciplined ear of his critic may well be called upon to let it pass.

Loewe is now more and more cultivated, but there are still many of his works unknown. They are like the hoard of the Nibelungen, hidden and guarded by the few. He who wants to recover these treasures of sublime art, must possess the wit and heroic energy of an ardent musical Siegfried, like Gura, Bulsz, Henschel, Vogel, Meyer, and Betz.

Let us hope that many more noble singers will, as priests of humanity, lovingly spread these ever-refreshing songs, that the whole world may learn to know

Loewe's genius, and appreciate and esteem his great merits. No doubt Loewe's ballads are no child's play, but if intelligent amateurs would study them with care and interest, they could do justice to a great many of his popular ballads, such as "Henry the Fowler," "Harald," "Edelfalk," "Der Fischer," "The Clock," and others. Loewe himself says: "My compositions demand a master on the piano, a great vocalist with clear pronunciation and declamation; if the singer has these requisites at command, the spirit of the composition will soon wing its upward flight."

The great dramatic compositions of Loewe, such as the "Moorish Prince," "Edward," "Die Drei Lieder," "Oluf," "Erlking," "Hochzeitlied," and "Odin's Ride over the Sea," should only be performed by accomplished artists, as they require noble vocalisation, great compass, and much culture. Loewe's ballads, especially those with the words by Goethe, Schiller, Uhland, Rückert, and Herder, are classical compositions, and, if well performed, must have a beneficial influence on musical culture. I am therefore convinced that Loewe's ballads would also purify the taste of the people, which is degenerated through mediocre compositions, especially through the so-called "drawing-room ballads." I blame for this the artists who sing such bad compositions in public. The duty of an artist is to instruct and to cultivate the taste of the people, and to make them capable of understanding sublime works of art. He should only sing good music of sterling character, as nothing is so dangerous for art as mediocrity. A wise Indian says—

> "Bad is not the bad, as it very seldom deceives.
> Mediocrity is bad, as it may pass for good."

There are, unfortunately, publishers and concert-givers who believe that popular music is more profitable than classical music; but that is not true. The taste of the people will be changed in a short time if they are compelled to hear only good music, and it will soon have the same effect on the audience as the magnet on iron,—it will attract.

Vocalists and amateurs should, besides cultivating "art ballads," sing also the ballads of the people, and national songs which express the true feelings of the people. I believe all national songs are eternally good and vital; but most of the so-called drawing-room ballads, which are daily manufactured by dozens, and put under celebrated names into the market, are worthless, and of evil influence.

Some of Loewe's ballads which I sang in concerts I intend to publish with English and German words for a medium voice, with a few remarks concerning their expression and rendering, and I hope by such an edition to popularise his ballads.

At the Philosophical Institution I sang as illustrations Schubert's and Loewe's most popular ballads, " The Erlking" and " The Fischer," and asked the audience to decide who—Loewe or Schubert—deserves the palm for the ballad, as I thought the best critic in matters of art is an intelligent audience, and I was glad to observe that Loewe was victorious!

I give but a sketch of Schubert, the greatest songcomposer, as *he* is not a stranger in this country, and there are excellent biographies of him, which make a new one superfluous. I will only narrate what I heard four years ago, in my summer holidays, from his most intimate and still living friend Hofkapellmeister Benedikt Randhartinger, Vienna, concerning his celebrated " Müllerlieder," his " Erlking," and his financial difficulties. Most of these stories will be new to my readers, as they do not appear in Schubert's biography.

I cannot conclude this preface without expressing
my indebtedness to Frau Julie von Bothwell, eldest
daughter of Loewe, and to Dr M. Runze, President of
the Loewe Verein in Berlin, for the kindly aid and
valuable information which they have freely given
me.

ALBERT B. BACH.

13 CASTLE TERRACE,
EDINBURGH, 1st *July* 1890.

THE ART BALLAD

THE ART BALLAD.

After Bach, Handel, Haydn, Gluck, Mozart, and Beethoven had established the different forms in music and produced marvellous works in every branch, it seemed doubtful whether any other master could create a new form in music, when suddenly two heaven-born singers appeared—melodious Schubert in the south and daring Loewe in the north of Germany; and with their first compositions all doubts vanished. Schubert was the creator of the art song, Loewe the creator of the art ballad. In Schubert's nature the lyric element was predominant, in Loewe's the dramatic.

There were indeed several distinguished composers before Schubert who composed lyrical songs. I need only mention Johann Fr. Reichardt (1752-1814), Carl

Fr. Zelter (1758-1832), Joh. Rud. Zumsteeg (1760-1802), Joh. Wolfgang Mozart (1756-91), and Ludwig van Beethoven (1770-1827). These all lived during a period when Goethe's lyric poems exercised a magic power over Germany, and when every composer exercised his talent in setting his songs to music.

Reichardt was best known through his settings of Goethe's poems, of which he composed sixty. He was a highly cultured musician, but without much creative power.

Zelter was the son of a mason in Berlin. In early boyhood he showed much talent for music. He was an intimate friend of Goethe and Fichte, and teacher of Mendelssohn. His correspondence with Goethe, published in six volumes, is most interesting. For the lyric of Goethe he found a somewhat warmer tone; but he, as well as Reichardt, moved in too limited a sphere of thought, and was not able to do full justice to the sensitive faculty of Goethe's lyric. Goethe himself said that he preferred the compositions of Zelter to all others, especially because he put as little music as possible to his poems.

Zumsteeg was on terms of friendship with Schiller, with whose great and noble mind he sympathised. In

1792 he was director of the opera in Stuttgart, and
through his compositions he soon became the favourite
of the public. His ballads are melodious, and largely
formed after Mozart. They are written in a singing
style, with the simplest accompaniments, but they
have rather the form of the romance. Loewe was a
great admirer of his compositions, but nowadays these
have vanished from the platform. Zumsteeg had a
strong will but little imagination, and not much talent;
he could not create anything which would live for
all time.

Mozart, in his charming songs "The Violet," "To
Chloe," and others, has fertilised Schubert's imagination.
Beethoven, in his beautiful "Knowest thou that dear
Land," "Adelaide," and "Neue Liebe neues Leben," has
bequeathed excellent songs to the world. In Mozart's
as well as in Beethoven's compositions the words have
found more consideration, and have more influenced
the form and expression of the music, than in those
of the other composers just mentioned; but we must
admit that they were not destined to discover the true
form for the art song.

Mozart and Beethoven were composers of too mighty
calibre, and had tasks too important to perform, to be

able to accommodate their power to the limited domain
of song. They employed their faculties for greater
problems, giving their imagination wider scope, and
they regarded the song as a mere accessory. Reichardt, Zelter, and Zumsteeg, on the other hand, adhered
too closely to the national song, and the pianoforte
accompaniments they wrote are only subordinate, sub-
serving the melody without aiming at the higher purpose of emphasising the expression of the song by
means of the accompaniment, and of thus elevating
the hearer into a higher sphere of enjoyment.

Schubert alone succeeded in extending the domain
of musical expression in a manner previously unknown, and in creating melodies of inimitable sweetness. In his twentieth year he had already discovered
the concise and genuine form of the art song, in which
he interpreted and poetised anew the whole lyric of
Goethe with marvellous skill, thus delighting his
countrymen with a new and glorious spring-tide of
national song. In a word, Schubert was at once the
creator and the king of the modern art song.

What is it, then, that differentiates the art song
from the Volkslied?

The Volkslied is a song which originates among the

humbler classes, is sung by the people, and is handed
down by oral tradition. The Volkslied in its proper
sphere is the simple and artless expression of some
homely sentiment or mood, corresponding with one or
other of the psychological instincts. It is generally a
love-song, and is often inspired with charming sentiment. In an unsophisticated manner it gives utterance
to the whole range of the tender passions, beginning
with the yearning for a reciprocative object of awakening love, and passing from the first sweet emotions,
through all the trials of constancy, up to that love
which even death cannot sever. To the same class
belong the numerous German students' songs, patriotic
songs, and soldiers' songs—these last being usually at
the same time love-songs, from the tenor of which it
would almost seem as if a soldier, whether lancer, rifle-
man, or dragoon, were not conceivable without a sweet-
heart. Perhaps even in Scotland the same kind of
thing is not unknown.

The Volkslied usually appeals to the heart in the
most direct manner, and asserts its sway over uncul-
tured and refined alike. The songs of this class are,
moreover, generally associated with the most beautiful melodies, the creation of which necessarily pre-

supposes those strong emotions which animate even the humblest classes of the community.

All peoples, indeed, possessed beautiful national melodies long before artistic compositions were presented to them, and it is often in the truest and most touching accents that heartfelt love reveals itself in the simple songs of the people—

> " Du bist mein, und ich bin Dein ;
> Ach, was kann wohl schöner sein ?"

> " Thou art mine, and I am thine ;
> Ah, could there be aught so fine ?"

The words together with the tune constitute the Volkslied. Without the melody the Volkslied would be like a picture without colour. The words of a song arouse popular emotions only when actually sung.

Thanks to the labours of a number of poets and scholars, we are enabled to trace the German Volkslied from its origin in the fourteenth century to the zenith of its perfection in the fifteenth and sixteenth centuries, to its decline during the Thirty Years' War, to its revival in the eighteenth century, and to its abiding vigour at the present day.

The musicians of the sixteenth and seventeenth centuries collected a great many of these songs and preserved them from oblivion, and the most beautiful of them still live in the hearts of the people. The most eminent composers have delighted in them, but few have attained their touching simplicity: for one cannot but feel that the melody burst simultaneously with the words from one and the same inspiration. With the first notes of the tunes the words start to our lips; and again the spoken word involuntarily suggests the gentle flow of the melody. Of the same nature must all true lyrical poetry be, moving most potently the innermost soul.

In Germany, Johann Gottfried Herder (born in 1744) was the first to recognise the value of the popular lyrics of different nationalities. It was he who ventured to say to the poets of his time, " Listen to the Volkslieder of all nations ; let these be your teachers ; " and he has proved the soundness of his advice in his valuable ' Stimmen der Völker,' or collection of national songs from many parts of the world, which demonstrate that all peoples are capable of singing, of touching the heart, and of poetically representing their own lives. In compiling this collection, he gathered from ancient chronicles, from the accounts of travellers, and from the lips of the common people, the simplest and most beautiful songs of almost all known nationalities. Here we find the Spaniard singing under the balcony of his donna, the Sicilian fisherman invoking the Holy Virgin, the poor Laplander discoursing to his love on the faithfulness of his reindeer, or the musing Lithuanian maiden who hears in her harp, made of the wood of the linden - tree, the sighing of her departed sister's soul. He has proved, in short, that love and song *flourish* in every zone and clime.

It was Herder, too, who referred his young friend Goethe to the vast treasures of poetry preserved in the Volkslieder, which in those days received but scant attention. He wisely counselled him to lay aside Klopstock and Hagedorn—who were looked upon as models—and to roam through the woods and fields listening to the songs of the country folk, which would soon make him forget the bookish poets. Goethe took the hint, and fell to studying the Volkslieder with ardent zeal. He dived deep into their tuneful life, imbued himself with their spirit, and found in their simple forms the truest expression of feeling.

It is interesting to note that Goethe almost literally adopted the Volkslied of the "Haideröslein"—

> "Sah ein Knab ein Röslein stehen,
>   Röslein auf der Haiden"—

among his own lyrics. To this charming ditty Reichardt supplied a melody, and Schubert made use of the same tune,—both compositions being in E flat major and in $\frac{2}{4}$ time, though Schubert's accompaniment is richer. Yet this identical tune, with but little variation, had been sung by the people in much earlier times. Loewe, too, has in his ballads largely profited by the Volkslied, as, for instance, in "Harald," "Prinz Eugen," "Heinrich der Vogler," "Der Edelfalk," and others.

These, and many other songs, prove how much poets and composers alike have learned from the popular lays: they show that the chief lyric poet of Germany, the foremost composer of ballads, and the greatest songwriter in the world, each drew his noblest inspiration from the poetry of the people.

In the history of literature of more recent date a prominent place is devoted to the poetry of the people, for in it the true secret of poetic creation may be studied. We now possess, besides Herder's 'Voices of the Nations,' excellent collections of Volkslieder in Achim von Arnim and Clemens Brentano's 'Des Knaben Wunderhorn,' and in the compilations made by Uhland, by Hoffmann von Fallersleben, and by the gifted wife of Professor Edward Robinson, sister-in-law to Loewe, Carl Simrock (1851), and many others.

A few words may now be said regarding the musical construction of the Volkslied.

The Volkslied is always strophic — that is, the melody of the first verse is simply repeated in all the following verses. It is therefore evident that while the melody may convey or interpret the general purport of the poem, or express its actuating impulse or mood, it cannot adapt itself to the various changes of feeling expressed by the words of the different verses. The art song, on the other hand, is, as a rule, not strophic; the melody is not the same in all the verses, but the composition adapts itself to each new turn of feeling, so that each obtains its own special musical representation.

Observe also that the Volkslied is originally conceived as a mere melody, and if harmony is added, it is limited to an accompaniment in the simplest chords. The melody of the Volkslied usually consists of two short parts, similar to each other; the first leading from the tonic or key-note to the dominant or fifth, while the second leads back from the dominant to the tonic. Much less common is the transition of the melody to the subdominant or relative minor. The national songs which are written in the minor mode modulate either into the key of the relative major or into that of the dominant. Like the national dances, most national songs consist of a period of eight bars: it is understood that, if the national song consist of two or more parts, it will contain sixteen or more bars. There are Volkslieder which carry little melodic phrases up to the dominant or subdominant, and finish the song with one of these notes. This form is especially common among the Russian Volkslieder. Such incomplete endings, terminating as it were in the middle, do not, however, suit the more fully developed sense of melody of the German. He goes on developing the tune, and in consequence developing the poem, until the principal key is again reached. It is a noteworthy feature that where Germans are socially assembled, the whole company join in singing. Thus, for instance, in the meetings of students or soldiers, there is always a chorus, and owing to this and to the different pitch of the individual voices the result is part - singing; and in this part - singing, where the preponderance of the melody in the German national tunes is manifest, the whole leads without effort to harmony.

In the art song, again, the accompaniment makes itself felt independently and with an equal claim to attention. The result is the so-called "Tonmalerei," or painting in music. Here the accompaniment also materially serves to delineate more precisely the sentiment by means of contrasts occurring in the different stanzas. The form and modulation of the Volkslied are therefore extremely simple, while the art song, even when composed in strophic form, shows more expanded forms and richer modulations.

But to whatever class it belongs, genuine song is never the fruit of mere thought and toil; the profoundest knowledge of counterpoint avails nothing. Like the poet, the composer "is born, not made."

In order to compose an art song, it is indispensable that the composer should thoroughly realise the intention of the poet; nay, that he should so identify him-

self with the poem as almost to create it over again.
The spark that kindled the idea of the song in the
poet's breast must, so to speak, glow again with renewed
force in the composer's heart, and awaken along with
the words the tones which slumber in the musician's
soul like an all-embracing, all-controlling marvel. In
a moment of inspiration the intellectual conception,
which no cogitation or compilation could ever call
into existence, flashes forth spontaneously and glori-
ously. To achieve success, the music of the song must
thoroughly blend with the words, so that, to use the
happy phrase of Henry Purcell, Handel's great prede-
cessor, " the music and the poetry being wedded, it
may seem as if wit and beauty were united in one and
the same person." If, in short, the composer has succeeded in inventing a beautiful melody or in idealising
a national song by giving them respectively a characteristic harmonisation and form, combining feeling
with truth of expression and spirit with gracefulness,
he has satisfied all just demands, and has produced
an art song. The finest examples of the idealised
national song, both in strophic and " through composed" form, were created, after Schubert and Mendelssohn, by Schumann, Brahms, Robert Franz, Grieg

and Jensen, Sterndale Bennett, Gerard Cobb, Frederick
Cowen, and others.

Hoping that I have thus sufficiently indicated the
distinction between the Volkslied and the art song, I
shall now proceed to discuss the nature of the ballad.

Ballads are epic in character—that is, they depict
events and actions.   Their subjects are drawn either
from the world of spirits or from legend, from myth
or from history.   For the most part they are of a
grave or even gloomy cast, with predominating features of a demoniacal and fantastic nature.   The *dramatis personæ* rise before us on a background generally sombre, and the events of a ballad are as it were
enacted with dramatic vividness before our very eyes.
Often, too, the intervention of mysterious supernatural
beings, embodiments of the baneful powers of nature,
enhances the interest and fascination of the scene.
" The ballad," says Goethe, " requires a mystical touch,
by which the mind of the reader is brought into that
frame of undefined sympathy and awe which men
unavoidably feel when face to face with the miraculous
or with the mighty forces of nature."

The Germans owe a debt of gratitude to the Scotch
and the English for their ballads, for it was by these

that the poets of Germany were stimulated to cultivate this form of poetry, and in it to produce works of imperishable beauty. The ballad has revealed to us a new world; it has transported us into that realm of the marvellous where fancy reigns supreme.

Achim von Arnim and Clemens Brentano prefix a charming popular ballad to their collection. A young stranger, roaming through the world on his swift steed, arrives at the castle of the empress. He dismounts, approaches the throne, kneels before the empress and presents to her a horn of ivory richly decked with gems. The fairy of the seas sends this gift to the young princess as a prize for her purity of mind, her wisdom and beauty. She only needs to touch the horn and it gives forth the most glorious tones, sweeter than the song of birds, clearer than the sound of the harp, lovelier than woman's voice or the mermaid's song. The empress touches the wonderful horn, and forthwith the hall is filled with music of supernatural beauty. All the hearers are in raptures; but when the empress wishes to thank the strange youth he is gone, and is only seen disappearing in the distance.

In this fantastical poem the wonderful tones of the horn signify the ballad itself sounding forth from the depths of the people's mind, and spreading over the wide world by tradition, and on the wings of music. Ballads were originally poetical productions of the people. Just as we are ignorant of the authors of the Volkslied, so we cannot now discover the authors of these ballads of the people. We can only conjecture that they were originally improvised by persons endowed with a fertile imagination and highly emotional character. "All poetry," says Aristotle, "springs from improvisations." Long before literature was, ballads were. In all likelihood ballad poetry is a development of that primitive impulse to sing whatever may be said in a moment of emotion, that still exists among savage tribes. In old times ballads were probably both sung and recited. Motherwell, a great authority on ballad literature, says, "Not infrequently the story was both sung and said." While the authors and the age of the ballads are unknown, we know the mode of their preservation. In all countries the singer-minstrels were the preservers of the ballads. They had good memories, as they learned the ballads only through oral tradition; they gave great pleasure to the people, and filled the place of modern concert and operatic singers. Their honorarium, however, was very meagre, and they

were not much respected, especially in Scotland. In
the laws of the early Scottish kings, bards and
minstrels are mentioned along with vagabonds, fools,
and idle persons, to be scourged and burnt on
the cheek, unless they found some work by which
to live.

As in the case of the Volkslied, so in that of the
ballad, there has long existed among poets a growing
conviction that poetry must ever renew its vitality by
drawing from that copious original source which has
been discovered in the ballads of the people, and to this
conviction we owe various collections of such ballads.
Perhaps the finest of these collections is that of English
and Scottish ballads, published in 1765 by Bishop
Thomas Percy in his ' Reliques of English Poetry,' and
made known to the Germans by J. G. Herder and A. G.
Bürger (1748-94). Bürger especially received through
these English and Scottish ballads an impulse to poetical production of a similar nature, and so became the
originator of the German art ballad, to which he gave
a wider compass than the old ballads had, and which
he raised to dramatic vividness through the free use of
dialogue. His ballads, " The Wild Huntsman " and
" Leonore," have scarcely been excelled in musical ring

and sonorousness of language. Next to Bürger, Goethe and Uhland are to be considered masters in this line. Goethe in particular combines in his ballads great depth of thought with brisk and simple narrative. The more intimately he became acquainted with the old popular ballad, or, as we should rather call it, with the primitive poetry, the greater became his wonder and his reverential desire to find out the secret of the concentration within those ballads of the most widely divergent rays into so narrow a compass; and in his own ballads he accordingly strove to attain the greatest possible succinctness, suggesting rather than unfolding everything. He thus left room for the imagination both of the reader and of the composer, who have thus to supply what the poet does not choose to say, and in this way come to have a share in his work. It is certain that Goethe, in his "Erlking," surpassed the authors of the old ballads in tenderness and dramatic power, and created the most perfect model of an art ballad.

Schiller's conception of the ballad differs from that of Bürger in so far as Schiller treats his subjects with greater regard for detail, and is almost too particular, too full for musical treatment.

Uhland approaches Goethe in conciseness. Readers of an imaginative turn will admire in his ballads the healthy and beautiful fruit of romanticism. Uhland, writing in the spirit of Goethe, has succeeded in recalling to new life the middle ages, and has idealised them with his fertile imagination. We cannot help liking his knights and the fair ladies of the castle, and even sceptics are seized with a certain yearning when he makes the clear bells of his "lost church" (ballad "Verlorene Kirche") ring out again.

Among the many worthy disciples of these great masters may be mentioned Schwab, Platen, Zedlitz, Lenau, Chamisso, Heine, Vogl, Fontane, and Eichendorff. With this wealth of ballads presented to them, it was but natural that composers should try to set them to music; and no fewer than thirty-nine composers, of whom Reichardt was the first, have written settings of the "Erlking."

Those ballads which treat of ghost-stories have most of all attracted the composers, because within their domain of mystery imagination finds the widest scope. The "ghost ballads" are, like the fairy tales, relics of pagan mythology, and trace their origin to an age when man mainly lived in the midst of and busied himself with nature, when the human mind had a strong bent towards the miraculous, and when religion consisted in the worship of personified nature. The Christian Church pronounced sentence of banishment on the gods, but they could not be entirely ousted from the minds and memories of men. In the course of ages the gods degenerated into subordinate deities, and at length became transformed into good or evil spirits, who were either hostile to man or benignly disposed towards him. So we find the dwarfs who keep watch over the gold with which, like the rich of this world, they can work much evil or good. The elves dance in the moonlight and entice men—as, for instance, in " Herr Oluf "—to dance with them, upon which the men become seized with such an ecstasy of delight that they can never stop until they fall down dead. Stream and lake are tenanted by fair nymphs, by whose song and playing mortals are drawn, as in Goethe's " Fischer," down to watery death. All these spirits and demons play a great part in the ballad.

E. Schuré poetically exclaims: "Ye dark spirits of the mountains, ye elves in the woods, and ye playful nymphs in the clear lakes ! how is it that you still live and call to us with your plaintive voices?

Why have we not bidden you farewell for ever? It is because you so bewitchingly tell us of times when you ruled the world, and when man revered you. Then nothing had yet separated man from nature. Of nature was his first loving greeting, and you, nature's beings, have preserved the secret to bring back to him that enchantment. The Church has banned you; civilisation has supplanted you; the people who once loved you deride you, or have forgotten you. But we bear you, ye friendly deities, in affectionate remembrance. For involuntarily we return to nature to invigorate ourselves in its embraces, and to feel the eternal spirit that lives in all things. Then you live again for moments, and in your smiles we find once more the happiness of the golden age." Loewe has in a special sense renewed the life of these beings of the dark and mysterious past.

We shall now consider the musical treatment of the *romance* and of the *art ballad*.

The romance stands between the song and the ballad, but it is more lyric than dramatic. An event is narrated, but the narration is only casual, being called upon to give expression to the representation of some distinct psychological moment. The leading object of

the narration is to give scope to the lyric element, and
the event narrated is only considered in so far as it supports this leading object, as, for instance, in Goethe's
"The Violet" or "The King of Thule."

The romance, with all its tenderness and subjective
feeling, is less dramatic or passionate than the ballad,
and has a tendency to limit itself to a tranquil lyrical
tone. Another characteristic feature of the romance is
that it generally deals with the adventures and deeds
of knights, whilst the domain of the ballad is the
myth and the world of spirit. The musical treatment
of the romance, again, has more likeness to that of
the art song than that of the art ballad. There are
also instrumental works which have taken the form
of the romance; as in these the words are absent,
the music will have to represent the leading mood in
a more diversified and animated fashion. Models
of this form we find in Beethoven's two "Romances
for Violin." A fine example also occurs in Max
Bruch's "Romance for Violin," dedicated to Robert
Heckmann.

As to the word "ballad," we find in musical and
other dictionaries different explanations of it. Some
say it is derived from a song to be sung at a dance,

from the Italian *ballare*, to dance; others, that ballad is a sentimental song, a light poem, a lyric tale in verse, or a simple song, each verse being sung to the same tune; while others again say that it is a song designed to suit popular tastes, or a simple narrative of events set to a tune which might also be used for one of the original purposes of a ballad—namely, as a dance-tune.

There is no doubt that in olden times singing was used in order to regulate dancing. As with the Greeks the metre of their language has adapted itself exactly to the rhythm of the dance—nay, has even borrowed certain marks of expression and time from it—so a similar adaptation took place in other nations of old, with whom the national song was also in intimate relationship with the dance.

Every change of mood or temper demonstrates itself in the countenance, and especially in movements of the body; from these movements the dance originates. The happy mood reflects itself in livelier movements. We still find that people when dancing, marching, or working in company, in fields, forests, or gardens, like to sing; and it seems that this facilitates their work, making their yoke easier and their burden lighter. We

may therefore accept the different explanations mentioned, as they are more or less true in reference to the
ballads of the people, or even to the so-called modern
drawing-room ballads, as these are really simple songs,
each verse of which is, in the main, sung to the same
tune ; but the art ballad, as created by Loewe, demands
a different explanation.

Just as the art song has differentiated itself from the
Volkslied by becoming mainly a "through composed"
song, or song in which the melody continuously follows the changes of mood which occur in the different
verses of the poem, so the art ballad, as created by
Loewe, became a distinct thing from the simple old-
fashioned setting of the popular ballad. It differed from
the latter in its form. The composer's aim now was to
follow closely the poet's ideas, and to clothe them with
adequate and appropriate musical expression ; hence he
must needs possess a vivid imagination, and the rare
gift of mastering the dramatic, epic, and lyric elements
of his art ; for these three factors are essential constitu-
ents of the art ballad. In some art ballads the dramatic
element is predominant, in some the narrative is the
main thing ; but we find that even the narrative ballads,
such as " The Moorish Prince," " The Night Parade,"

&c., demand dramatic treatment, owing to the force and vividness of the story.

In the narrative ballads the composer must be careful not to fall into a dry, monotonous strain, nor must he neglect the lyrical elements; and he must, in all cases, be in full sympathy with the speaker or narrator who is generally introduced by the poet.

The interest of the hearers is largely sustained by the instrumental accompaniment, which generally finds additional scope for appropriate musical expression and treatment in the prelude, in occasional interlude, and in the postlude.

The music in most art ballads corresponds at the outset and towards the end with the plain narrative style of the poem; while in the action proper, given in the intermediate part of the ballad, it assumes a calm lyrical tone or an exciting dramatic character, corresponding with the nature of the story. In the same way the composer must distinctly individualise the persons who speak or act—as, for example, in the ballad of " Oluf," the narrator, the elves, Oluf's mother, and other characters. The music here does not, as in the song, merely express the general mood, but enters into details— represents, describes, paints—as developed by Loewe.

In the art ballad, therefore, the same tune is not given to all the verses, as is the case in the Volkslied and in the ballads of the people.

It is strange that none of the composers preceding Loewe should have known how to give to the ballad the proper musical tone—that is, to find the true narrative style. Reichardt treats the "Erlking" as a romance, and has for both the narrative and the speeches of the father and son one and the same ordinary song-melody. Zelter's ballads, " Der Jäger " and " Der Gott und die Bajadere," show a similar musical treatment. In Zumsteeg's " Ritter Toggenburg " and his celebrated " Leonore," the popular style of the romance forms the basis; and where he attempts tone-painting, and seeks to illustrate the narrative musically, he becomes somewhat tiresome, his colouring is rather insipid, and he fails to find the true tone of the narrator.

Neither for Reichardt nor for Zelter has the action any particular interest; they invent a melody for the first stanza, which is repeated in all the other stanzas, and undergoes but immaterial modifications where this is required by the altered declamation.

We find even the immortal Schubert, in his music to Goethe's ballad " Der Fischer," making no distinction

between the narrative and the speaking and singing
water-nymphs ; and we find him treating in a very elementary fashion the dramatic episodes in the celebrated
old Scottish ballad " Edward," called in Schubert's
songs " Eine altschottische Ballade " (translated by Herder), op. 165, as he uses only one melody for this grand
poem. On the other hand, Schubert has in Goethe's
" Erlking," and in Collin's " Der Zwerg " (The Dwarf),
given us most praiseworthy contrasts to this mode of
treatment.

The scene of action also must, so to speak, be rendered visible by the music to the hearer's eye. For
music has power, with its infinite combinations of
rhythm and tone-colour, to stimulate the imagination,
and thus cause it to shape forth places and scenes as of
the outer world.

Familiar examples of this descriptive music, or tone-
painting, are afforded by Hadyn's " Creation " and
Beethoven's " Pastoral Symphony "; and no one who
has heard Wagner's " Flying Dutchman," or his " Ride
of the Valkyries," or his " Fire-spell," can doubt that he
stands pre-eminent as a tone-painter. So Weber too,
in his " Oberon," marvellously well represents the merry
gambols of the elves, which Mendelssohn in his " Mid-

summer Night's Dream," and Schubert and Schumann, have also most charmingly rendered in their respective manners. I do not, however, believe that any composer previous to Wagner has painted with so rich and brilliant effect as Loewe has done.

In order fully to appreciate the effects of tone-painting, the hearer must, of course, also possess a plastic imagination, so as to be able readily to grasp and follow the composer's intentions. Imagination must here assist the ear as it assists the eye, when we fancy we see mountains, figures, landscapes, and strange forms in the clouds.

The various elements we have here considered—the narrative, the lyrical, the dramatic, and the descriptive elements in their due proportions—constitute the art ballad; and it was Loewe who first fully understood, and with a master-hand carried out, this principle. He elevated the ballad into what I would call a musical drama in miniature; and in indicating for it the æsthetic principle of the unity of the epic, the lyric, and the dramatic elements, he created the model for all future productions of the kind.

JOHANN KARL GOTTFRIED LOEWE

JOHANN CARL GOTTFRIED LOEWE.

JOHANN CARL GOTTFRIED LOEWE, the greatest of ballad composers, was born 30th November 1796, in Lobejün, near Halle. His epoch was the epoch of the Ballad in its highest form. In the year of his birth Schiller and Goethe wrote a great many of their finest ballads, which were published in the following year in the 'Musenalmanach,' which is therefore called the 'Balladen Almanach.'

Loewe's father was a schoolmaster and choirmaster: he initiated his son in the mysteries of his art, and kindled his enthusiasm for the beautiful. The father, Andreas Loewe, had been a pupil at the Grammar-school of Halle, and under his able guidance the musical talent of the boy was early and rapidly developed. Loewe himself says about it: "When I first became conscious of myself, I knew how to play the piano and the organ, and could sing at sight without being able to remember how I had learned these things, without even the slightest exertion." By the fairy tales, legends, and poetic recitations with which his gifted mother amused him during the winter evenings, his imagination was early awakened and fertilised, while he took great delight in the beautiful melodies she played to him on the violin. The recitation by one of his sisters of the then newly published ballads of Bürger greatly inspired him; and a brother, who had acquired under Righini a familiarity with the method of singing, instructed Loewe, and initiated him into the secrets of the old Italian school.

The parents of the little *virtuoso* allowed him every liberty in the use of his time, which he largely employed in roaming through his native plains, where his active imagination found ever new nourishment in field and grove, beside the brook and on the moor. It was to this refreshing and unrestrained open-air life that he owed that strong enthusiastic admiration for and intimacy with nature which is so frequently manifested in his compositions, and by which these exercise so great and peculiar a charm over every one who has in his youth dreamed at the bosom of the great mother and felt her beauty. Besides, the mind of the boy—who in his unhindered rambles was fond of associating with hunters, herdsmen, and fishermen, in order to gather from them many a tale of spectres of the woods, hobgoblins, and water-fairies—early received a poetical turn, with a predominant tendency to the romantic, which easily explains his subsequent predilection for the ballad.

In his tenth year Loewe was sent to the school of Köthen. Köthen is a charming place, open like a garden, the luxuriant vegetation of which delights the eye,—and it is especially interesting to the friends of music, from the fact that the great Sebastian Bach here spent his happiest years, under the auspices of the art-loving Duke of Anhalt-Köthen. Here Loewe's fresh soprano voice was often heard ringing out as clear as a bell in the church choir, and by his enchanting singing he soon won all hearts for himself. Loewe, in his 'Autobiography,' says of this time: "The people in the little town of Köthen admired and made much of me, as the public of large cities admire and like to make much of the great artists of the stage. We in our choir

were for them the representatives of the art; it was we
who beautified with our singing their devotion, and
nobly adorned it."

Having after three years gone through the highest
class of the school in Köthen, he became a pupil at the
Gymnasium of the Orphanage in Halle. Who does not
know Halle, where great Handel was born? It was
with reverence and a certain awe that Loewe ap-
proached the old university town. Immediately on his
arrival his father accompanied him to Professor Türk,
before whom he had to pass an examination and to
compose most difficult themes, as well as to read at
sight. The professor recognised the boy's musical
talent with the words, " God knows, the lad is a blade !
He can sing that at sight !" The severest test for his
musical ear still remained. Türk successively struck a
number of notes on the piano, which the boy was to
name without looking at the instrument. At his own
home Loewe had often done this with accuracy and
ease. On this occasion, however, he named not the
note struck, but always the third above it. Türk
quietly continued for a short time in his examination, and then turning to Loewe's father, said: " Herr
Cantor, your piano must be pitched a third below

mine ; your boy persists in naming the notes I touch
a third above." And it was actually the case that
Loewe's piano stood a third lower than that of the
professor. It may seem strange that even at the
beginning of the nineteenth century so great a dis-
crepancy in the pitch of pianos should have occurred
in Germany. Yet one must believe that it was so,
seeing that Loewe himself makes the statement.

The worthy professor took the most friendly interest
in the boy, instructed him carefully in the art of singing
and in the theory of music ; and Loewe always was a
welcome guest in his house, where his musical talent
found the most generous support. Soon Loewe was
counted among the best singers of Halle. One of his
most favourite parts was " The Queen of Night," from
Mozart's " Il Flauto Magico," which he knew how to
sing excellently, in spite of the extraordinary difficulties
it offers.

In those days it was still the fashion in Halle for the
young scholars to sing in the streets before the houses
of the wealthy in order to collect money ; the boys'
choir was never absent from weddings or funerals ; and
of the contributions so obtained, Professor Türk received
the tenth part. Halle had then (1810) no public artistic

establishment, and Türk's concerts were the only thing
offered for the enjoyment of art. " One day," Loewe
relates in his ' Autobiography,' " the Chancellor Nie-
meyer asked Türk to give a vocal entertainment in
the hall of the Hotel ' Zum Kronprinzen.' In the
hall there was a lady who came forward and ad-
dressed me affably in French. Fortunately she herself was talking in so animated a manner that I
was spared the embarrassment of making a reply.
So much, however, I succeeded in gathering from
her most rapidly delivered speech that she had been
pleased with my singing, and that she wished me
success in my future career. I stood full of respect before her when the Chancellor said to me in
German, ' Do not forget this hour, my son, and remember that you have stood before Madame de
Staël ; ' and then the lady pressed an eight-groschen
piece into my hand. To my shame I must confess that
the silver coin, which in those times had for me the
value of a great treasure, made a deeper impression on me than the celebrated donor herself. I
had never troubled myself about the great minister
Necker and his daughter ; and while Schiller had a few
years previously sighed under the gushing conversa-

tion of this Madame de Staël, I got off, thanks to my
youth, with a short reply and my eight-groschen piece."

Halle at that time belonged to the so-called kingdom
of Westphalia, and stood under French dominion. King
Jerome, the brother of Napoleon I., acted the part of a
sovereign, and when he visited Halle in 1810 Loewe
had often an opportunity of singing before him. The
king expressed much pleasure in his performances, and
granted him, for the purpose of completing his musical
studies, the then quite extraordinary allowance of 300
thalers per annum from the revenue of the country.

Türk, who was also the teacher of the renowned
musical *littcrateur* and theoretician, Adolf Bernhard
Marx, thereupon gave Loewe, during the years 1811-
13, several lessons daily both in the theory of music
and in composition. At the commencement of his lessons Türk required Loewe to write a great concert aria
for a soprano voice. A friend of Loewe's selected a
classical subject for it — viz., "Didone abandonata."
The words were—

> " Der Troer hat mein Herz bezwungen,
>   Erloschen ist des Gatten Bild,
>   Tief ist der Pfeil ins Herz gedrungen,
>   Die Liebesflamme lodert wild!"

"I composed the air in an animated *tempo*," says Loewe. "It was in D minor, and quite short; there was much ecstasy, but neither in the words nor in the music was there any repetition. It did not seem natural to me that a despairing woman who is on the point of throwing herself into the flames should repeat her words."

C. H. Bitter, Prussian ex-Minister of Finance, and author of several works on the science of music, very correctly observes in his treatise on Loewe's Autobiography, that Loewe in this respect anticipated Richard Wagner, who is well known to have followed similar principles. When Loewe brought Türk his aria, the professor looked at the music and smiled. "What is written here is very good," said he, "but now the real aria ought to begin." Loewe shook his head. "Ay, ay," said the master; "this is good music, but no aria!" "Then I shall write another one," replied Loewe; "but this one must remain as it is." And Türk had to consent, because he knew that Loewe, notwithstanding his child-like inexperience, would not alter anything once written. Loewe himself says: "I never liked altering in my compositions. Many a thing in them left much to be desired; yet as the manuscript once stood it had to remain. It was always impossible for me to alter even a single note."

In 1813 the downfall of Jerome's kingship and Türk's death altered Loewe's plans. His youth and the condition of his health, weakened by severe study, precluded him from the much-desired participation in the war of liberation. So he returned to the Gymnasium of Halle, where in the meantime his fellow-pupils had far outstripped him. A noble ambition, however, urged him to such energetic efforts that he was able to enter the university in 1817. To the zeal with which he here prosecuted his studies we owe the depth and truthfulness with which he in later times grasped and pictured the life of the Old and New Testaments in his vocal oratorios, and in his settings of Lord Byron's "Hebrew Melodies." Altogether, Loewe acquired during these years that superior philosophical refinement which is manifested so largely in the spirit of his compositions and other productions, and without which in our times no artist has much chance of achieving a reputation. Loewe once said, "Genuine art must be rooted in the soil of philosophical culture."

About this time a Vocal Quartett Association was
formed in Halle under the leadership of Adolf B. Marx.
This circle had a special attraction for Loewe; for one
of its members, the one who took the soprano parts,
was a young lady of rare and fascinating gifts. She,
who afterwards became Loewe's wife, was Julie von
Jacob, a daughter of the meritorious Privy Councillor
von Jacob, professor of jurisprudence and political
economy. Having been brought up amid surroundings
calculated to awaken the most generous aspirations
after everything pure, noble, and beautiful, she possessed a clear discernment and natural appreciation of
art. "These qualities," says Loewe, "made a profound
impression upon my youthful heart. I soon enough
felt that it was no mere student's flirtation that was
beginning to live and to glow there, and eagerly
watched the signs of the growth of a similar feeling
on her part."

The membership of Marx's Quartett Association increased almost daily, so that soon oratorios by Handel,
Haydn, and others were executed with pianoforte
accompaniments. In these oratorios Loewe sang the
tenor solos. Later on, also, operas by Gluck and
Spontini were undertaken, especially such as the

members had no opportunity of hearing on the stage.
But what most delighted Loewe was Mozart's "Requiem."
This circle afforded Loewe the most pleasing recollections in after-years; but there was another one that
became of far higher importance for him, through the
intellectual impulses and interchange of ideas it offered.
The members met once a-week, on the Friday evenings,
at the house of Professor Jacob. Here all the new
productions in the domain of literature and art were
discussed. What a treat it was for Loewe to follow
the conversation of Julie von Jacob with Marx, who
had made himself indispensable in this society by his
uncommon intellectual culture, and by his intimate
acquaintance with the arts and with music, as also by
all those excellent qualities he combined in his person!
In this circle one would meet all the foreign personages
with whom the famous university town then abounded,
and Englishmen, Russians, Dutchmen, and Americans
were here hospitably received.

Professor Jacob's three daughters were also great
attractions. One of these was Therese Amalie Louise
von Jacob, afterwards married to Professor Edward
Robinson of New York, and who achieved so high
a reputation as a poetess and writer on the litera-

tures and folk-lores of various foreign nationalities under the *nom de plume* of " Talvj," which she formed of the initials of her maiden name.

The second daughter, Emilie von Jacob, possessed a soprano voice of rare softness, richness, and feeling; yet for Loewe the voice of her sister Julie, quickened by a high intellectuality, had the greater charm.

Art and learning, intellectual stimulus in every direction, and an animating friendly intercourse—all had a most favourable and quickening influence on Loewe's career. Nor did he neglect athletic exercise; and besides the practice of the foil—never wanting in a German student's lodgings—that of swimming was eagerly kept up, and enabled him to rescue two persons from drowning.

In his second year at the university (1818) he composed his first two ballads, " Edward " and the " Erlking." A. B. Marx was so impressed by this new form of composition that he published them on his own account.

Dr Keferstein, in his ' Recollections,' very feelingly refers to a young man in plainest regimentals, who, especially when he sang the then newly written ballads, enraptured every hearer. This young man was our

artist, whose genius in those days shone forth with
more and more powerful and splendid rays. While
attending his university classes he was also serving
his year as a volunteer in the Prussian ranks. He
was, however, relieved from the severer duties of a
soldier while he imparted musical instruction to a
rifle corps. This gave Loewe an opportunity of ac-
quiring that experience in the handling of choruses
for male voices which is manifested in his later
works.

Among his university friends, Loewe especially excited the enthusiastic admiration of musicians of the
first order by his unexcelled, smooth, and expert rendering of the most difficult airs, the accompaniment to
which he played himself, and it was thereby that he
won the heart of his future wife. Dr Keferstein states
that he never, either before or afterwards, heard
Mozart's and other duets executed with warmer expression than by this couple united by the inspirations
of youthful love, but whose beautiful matrimonial
alliance was destined to be of so short a duration.
Following his love to Dresden, and residing there in
1819-20, Loewe enjoyed in a great measure the attention and kindly interest of C. M. von Weber, whose

E

permanent friendship he gained during a later visit.
Weber gave his first concert at Halle, where he performed some of his compositions for the piano, when
Loewe, as he modestly observes, had the honour of being
allowed to turn the leaves for him. At a second visit
Loewe introduced his affianced, and met with the most
amiable reception. On one of the evenings spent at
Weber's house, Loewe was playing the master's sonata
in A flat, when Frau von Weber entering the room, exclaimed: " Ah, I thought it was you who were playing, dear husband!" and Loewe felt quite proud at
this mistake. Loewe relates that Weber was a devout
Roman Catholic. At his bedside hung a crucifix and
several images of saints. He often went on his knees
in front of his conductor's desk during High Mass,
and kept the hearers waiting; yet they willingly
waited, for they knew Weber was in prayer.

When Loewe was a visitor at Weber's house he was
busy with his opera " Der Freischütz," and the writer
of the beautiful libretto, Fr. Kind, as well as Ludwig
Tick, were welcome friends at the tea-table. Once
Weber asked them whether Agathe was to fall a
victim at the conclusion of the drama. The friends
decided in favour of a tragic issue and Agathe's death.

Yet this opinion was not in harmony with Weber's religious sentiments, and he accordingly adopted the conclusion of the opera as at present always performed, maintaining against the views of his friends that a tragic end would violate the feelings of the audience, and leave them without a sense of consolation. The name of the opera was then "The Hunter's Bride." These happy days at Weber's house came but too soon to an end. Loewe had to return to Halle, and now lived there sweetening his work with happy recollections and dreams of the future.

In Halle he often sang Zumsteeg's ballads, especially Bürger's "Leonore" and Schiller's "Ritter Toggenburg." He says: "The music of this old and unjustly slighted master always deeply moved me. Its motives are characteristic and ingenious; they follow the poem with perfect fidelity, but they are mostly of an aphoristic nature. I fancy," he continues, "that the music ought to be more dramatic, and should have been worked out with more fully elaborated motives, somewhat in the style in which I have tried to write my ballads."

Loewe served his time in the Halle rifle battalion, in which he is said to have been the best marksman; but he

was relieved from all subsequent service by his august
patron the Crown Prince — afterwards Frederick
William IV. of Prussia—who did not wish Loewe's
hands to be spoiled by handling the rifle. Thus Loewe
finished his military service in one year.

In 1820 Loewe accepted an invitation to Jena from
his college friend Dr Keferstein, the author of a
novel, 'König Myes von Fidibus,' in which Loewe
played a principal part as Leo Tonleben. The strange
title of this novel (King Mouse of Pipe-match) ori-
ginated from the following incident: In Loewe's
little piano, by the aid of which he used to write
his compositions, a mouse had taken up its quarters,
and always came slipping out when Loewe began to
play, apparently listening with great attention. This
peculiar fancy of the little creature had suggested the
title of the novel. Dr Keferstein was very musical,
and a distinguished journalist; he wrote many articles
for the musical periodical 'Caecilia,' published by
Schott, and a short but excellent biography of Loewe
for Schelling's 'Musical Encyclopedia.'

Loewe, who entertained the greatest admiration for
Goethe, felt it impossible to leave Jena without having seen that prince of poets. Goethe occupied dur-

ing that summer a house in the Botanical Garden.
Loewe sent in his name as "studiosus Loewe from
Halle," and was shown into the garden.   Shortly
before this Kotzebue had fallen at Mannheim through
the dagger of C. L. Sand, a student impelled by a
fanatical enthusiasm for the liberty of Germany; and
when now Loewe was made to wait a considerable
time in the garden, he perceived that he was being
watched by some person in Goethe's parlour.   Loewe
thought to himself, "Can it be possible that people
there are looking on me with suspicion because I
am a student, and as such held to be a dangerous
individual ?   I believe I was looking innocent enough
then with my fair hair.   Besides, the roll of my music
to Goethe's 'Erlking' could be seen peeping out of
my pocket, and indicating my harmless errand.   At
length I was asked to go forward, and ushered into
the oblong drawing-room.

" Goethe was exceedingly kind, and while walking
up and down with me, conversed pleasingly about the
nature of the ballad.   Meanwhile, the servant kept
his post at the threshold of the door ; and it was
only after our conversation had gone on for a considerable time that Goethe motioned to him, and we

were left alone. I told him that I liked the ballad
above all other forms of poetry, and how the popular
legend of the 'Erlking,' in the grand and romantic
garb of his poem, had quite captivated me; so much
so, indeed, that I could not help setting it to music.
I considered the 'Erlking' to be the best of German
ballads—for this reason, that the characters represented
in it were all introduced in dialogue. 'There you are
right,' said Goethe. And I, made more and more
confident, added: 'Of your dramatic works I hold
"Tasso" to be the best. I have read it over and over
again, and always with renewed rapture.' 'I knew
that,' replied Goethe, 'before you said so.' And now
I asked his permission to sing the 'Erlking' to
him. 'I have, unfortunately, no piano here,' said
Goethe, with sincere regret, 'and I am the more sorry
for it, as I always feel better able for work after hearing music; but come to see me in Weimar. There I
have a musical evening every Friday, and I should
be glad to hear my poem there, with your music.'"[1]
It was unfortunately not in Loewe's power to avail
himself of this invitation; for when Loewe, several
years later, returning from a musical festival on the

---

[1] See Loewe's 'Autobiography,' p. 79.

Rhine, passed through Weimar, Goethe had died. But
eighteen years afterwards Walther von Goethe—the
poet's eldest grandson and special favourite—became
Loewe's pupil in the theory of music and composition,
and his intimate friend.

From Jena Loewe went directly to Berlin, in order
to undergo a musical examination before Zelter,
the director of the Singakademie. The municipality
charged Zelter with this task, and at his house Loewe
was for eight days hospitably entertained. The Academy was in possession of Joh. Seb. Bach's score of
the St Matthew's Passion-music, which at that time
had not yet been printed, and was not publicly known.
Zelter made Loewe sing the difficult tenor part of the
work before the assembled academy, whereupon Zelter said: "Indeed the pupils of Professor Türk know
how to sing." Loewe had then to play on the organ,
and to compose three fugues on themes given to him
by Zelter. The examination was a brilliant success.
Loewe was appointed to the post of choirmaster at
St Jacob's, where, in the capacity of a student of
theology, we find him for some time taking clerical
duty, and preaching sermons. He was appointed
teacher in the Gymnasium of Stettin, and married

his beloved Julie in September 1821. The excellent
work he did in his new spheres of action had even in
a single year the result that he was promoted to the
office of music director in St Jacob's Church, with
twice his former salary; and we also find him teach-
ing scientific subjects as well as music, both in the
Gymnasium and the College. In this environment,
which was, however, not favourable to his creative
genius, he laboured for forty-six years, with all the
energy of his ardent spirit, for the improvement of the
civic musical institutions. He started a great vocal
association, and deserved well of the whole province,
through the training of excellent pupils in the Normal
College; while he likewise set himself to the publication of a series of works, which soon spread his
fame beyond the borders of the land. Loewe was a
splendid organist, and the beautiful grand organ in
St Jacob's Church, which the inhabitants of Stettin
treasured as a relic of the pre-Reformation times, was
to him an object of special interest. Loewe says of it:
" I have from my first day in office loved this organ
of the venerable church, with its mighty and tender
voices, as one loves a beautiful human soul, in the
depth of which one may trustingly lay down one's

joy and sorrow, and in which one finds sympathy, consolation, and peace." To his pupils he used to say: " One must speak gently to a woman ; and so one may not smite St Cecilia in the face, and yet the sound the hand elicits must be rich and powerful."

In leisure hours he was always most kindly welcomed in the family of Professor Gassmann, with whom he ascended the observatory for the purpose of astronomical study. Even as a boy he had watched the starry firmament with a keen interest, and now he found in Gassmann an excellent instructor, and was quite delighted to be able to contemplate with him the wonders of the heavens. From this time he prosecuted astronomical studies with great zeal, and would say, " This is a science that lifts us far away over worlds and through distant space into the infinity and majesty of creation." Besides his astronomical observations, he carried out some mathematical investigations into the longitudinal and lateral vibrations of the monochord. He also, together with Gassmann, investigated the compass of notes reaching up to a height at which they can no longer be heard, but may be made visible.

These animating and congenial pursuits were interrupted in 1823, to his deep distress, by the death of

his beloved wife, after a union of only one year and
a half; and he was thrown into a state of mind of
which the compositions of the following years bear the
sad impress. It was then that he composed from Lord
Byron's Hebrew Melodies "Herod's Lament for Mariamne," a masterpiece one can scarcely hear without
being moved to tears, and for which I am anxious
to win the sympathies of my readers. Loewe wrote
to his friend Bruyck,—"But one composes such things
with one's own heart-blood!" Loewe had engraved on
the tombstone of his beloved Julie the words, "Blessed
are the pure in heart, for they shall see God." He
often visited this place so sacred to him, and every
blade of grass that sprang from the silent tomb seemed
to him to be a greeting from her. He lived almost
two sad years in cheerless loneliness; then one day an
engaging young lady, Auguste Lange, was ushered in,
to ask him to give her a course of singing lessons.
The beautiful soprano voice of his pupil, her talent for
painting, and still more, her noble-mindedness, awakened Loewe's interest, and once more he was a happy
man when she consented to become his wife—a consort
who sought her happiness in smoothing for him the
path on which he was further to follow his calling as

an artist. Her splendid vocal accomplishments became the charm of his oratorios, in which she took the high soprano parts, while Loewe sang the tenor.

The gratifying change in the composer's life and feelings soon showed itself in several larger works. His celebrated oratorio, "The Destruction of Jerusalem," op. 30, which he completed within a short time, met with an extraordinarily favourable reception upon its performance in Stettin in 1830, and even more so in Berlin in 1832, where it was conducted by his friend, the great composer G. L. P. Spontini, and Loewe was honoured by King Frederick William with a precious gift.

Among the persons in Stettin in whose house Loewe was received as a welcome guest, were the widow of Privy Councillor Tilbein, one of the most intellectual ladies in that city, and the family of Bishop Ritchel. At the house of Frau Tilbein he had first been presented to the then Crown Prince Frederick William. After his accession, the king also honoured the house of Field-Marshal von Wrangel with his presence; and in all these families Loewe had the opportunity of singing his ballads to the art-loving monarch, who enjoyed the performances so much that he frequently commanded

his attendance at Court at Potsdam. Here Loewe had,
on one occasion, to remain for eight days, in order to
sing his ballads to the king every evening.

Loewe's intimate friend, the professor and poet, L.
Giesebrecht, gave the impulse to several of his greater
compositions. Among these may be named "The Brazen Serpent," op. 40, a vocal oratorio for male voices;
"The Seven Sleepers," op. 46; "The Apostles of Philippi," op. 48, a vocal oratorio for male voices; and
"Gutenberg," op. 55, an oratorio in three divisions, for
the inauguration of the Gutenberg statue at Mayence,
which latter created a great sensation in that city as
well as in Leipzig. "The Brazen Serpent" was a decided success in Jena and in many other cities. "The
Apostles of Philippi" was recognised by an eminent
musical critic as the greatest and sublimest of all compositions for male voices. In Jena, where Loewe conducted the work himself, great homage was paid to him,
and he rejoiced to see that this new form created by
him was received with enthusiasm even by the public
at large.

Of several other oratorios written by Loewe in
course of time, we may mention "Palestrina," "Master of Avis," and "Huss," op. 82. Some musicians

assign a higher place to his oratorios than to his ballads. It is certain that in the oratorio he created new forms, and struck into new paths. Wellmer rightly says: "Many of his oratorios are musical dramas in oratorio form,"—a form which has influenced many modern composers.

"The Destruction of Jerusalem" (which I hope will soon be translated into English) is a work of great dimensions, and belongs to the category of modern dramatic oratorio—a form which has been adopted and developed by Franz Liszt in his "Cecilia" and "Elisabeth," and by Schumann in his "Paradise and Peri." Space does not allow me to go into detail in analysing this and others of Loewe's great oratorios, and I only wish to direct the attention of the public and conductors to this new source of study and culture. The grand instrumental preludes and intermezzos, the characteristic recitatives, the fine airs and choruses in "The Destruction of Jerusalem," may serve as models to modern composers. The last chorus is an extraordinarily fine fugue, which amply demonstrates Loewe's mastery in counterpoint; it is based on the following interesting subject:—

"The Awakening of Lazarus" (with German and English words), composed for a small choir and organ, contains several beautiful solos for soprano, alto, and bass, full of devotional feeling. The choruses, if not very striking, have fine harmonies, especially the first chorus, "Death, sin, life, grace." The Hallelujah

Chorus, " O wondrous deed!" is very effective; and most interesting and characteristic is the musical illustration of the scene where the stone is lifted up from Lazarus's grave.

Grave (mit vollen Stimmen, ohne Mixturen).

C 8.
Ganzes Pedal der Orgel, Posaune 16 u. 32 fuss.

The syncopated accompaniment, ascending in chromatic progression, and affording a fine crescendo, expresses in a very dramatic fashion the longing of Jesus to see His heavenly Father answer His ardent prayer. The choruses, admirably sung by several members of Mr Kirkhope's Choir in my Edinburgh Loewe concert, were warmly received by the audience.

Schumann in his 'Gesammelte Schriften,' p. 299, uses the following expression with regard to Loewe's prin-

ciple: " His new oratorio ' Huss ' (op. 82) follows in its
tendency the line of dramatic composition.   Even the
author of the words—Professor Zeune of Berlin—has
not meant it for the Church.   By some writers the
whole species of these works of art has been objected
to.   But is the application of music to be entirely with-
held from characters like Huss, Gutenberg, Luther,
Winkelried, and other champions of the faith or of
liberty, because they are not suitable subjects for the
opera or for the Church ?   The purely Biblical oratorio
cannot suffer in the least from such application.   But
we may well be glad that history has still many a great
figure to show which music needs only to appropriate
in order to expand its effects in a new direction, and
to lend them speech.   Loewe, too, seems to be most
deeply penetrated with this idea, since he does not
give up pursuing the line he has once taken.   As to
the composer's [Loewe's] capacity, the world has pronounced long since.   But there are many ways, and
Loewe has chosen a difficult one.   May he never weary
in it!—and even though he does, his must remain the
merit of having fought in the front ranks, striving
towards a new goal."

The " Brazen Serpent " and the "Apostles of Philippi"

are written as purely vocal oratorios for male voices; and only in a few passages does he supplement the chorus in accordance with the situation by the introduction of instrumental music.

Zelter's successor, Ed. Grell, said that he placed so high a value on Loewe's oratorios because he found them combining three enviable qualities—viz., spirit, inventive power, and grace. Although himself recognised as an eminent master in the field of sacred composition, he took pride in the fact that under his direction seven different oratorios of Loewe were executed by the Berlin Singakademie. H. Bellermann, in Crysander's 'Musik Zeitung,' places Loewe's "Huss" above Mendelssohn's "St Paul." The distinguished musical historian and critic, A. Ambros, on the other hand, thinks many parts of "Huss" rather studied—an opinion in which I cannot concur. Without discussing the relative merits of the two works, I would only observe that, when Loewe was engaged in his arduous official duties as choirmaster and professor, he wrote in one year two oratorios and twenty ballads, and he could not possibly have spared much time for subtilising and retouching. Moreover, Loewe was not in the habit of doing so. Perhaps it would have been to

F

the advantage of some portions of his work if he had
refined. Of many parts in the oratorio, " The Seven
Sleepers," Ambros fully approves; and to my gratifica-
tion I find him again using the expression, " One would
have to seek a long time to find anything more beautiful." According to L. Köhler's verdict, pronounced on
the occasion of the performance of " The Seven Sleepers "
at Königsberg in 1883, this work is a masterpiece that
must deeply impress every musician. " The Seven
Sleepers " was published in America in three English
translations, and performed with much success in
Boston, New York, and Philadelphia. It is to be
hoped that some of Loewe's oratorios may ere long
be taken up in this country by choral associations.
Loewe also exerted himself as a writer on music.
His ' Theory of Singing' appeared in a second edition
in 1828; and he also wrote a guide for the piano,
a book on counterpoint, and a commentary on the
second part of Goethe's ' Faust,' published by Logier
in Berlin in 1834, besides contributing a number of
articles to various musical periodicals.

Loewe's extraordinary gift of improvisation deserves
special mention. He very often asked in concerts for
poems, and set them at once to music. In this way

he composed his music to Goethe's "Zauberlehrling" in one of his concerts in Berlin.

In 1832 the University of Greifswald bestowed upon him, in consideration of his many services to art, the honorary degree of Doctor of Philosophy (Ph.D.); and later on he was appointed Fellow of the Royal Society of Fine Arts in Berlin.

Loewe had an interesting correspondence with some of the most prominent men of his time—for example, Fr. Rückert, Spontini, G. Weber, W. von Goethe, Prince Radziwill, Frau Handel Schütz, Th. Hildebrandt of Düsseldorf, who painted his portrait, Ed. Grell, and others. He was also on terms of friendship with the poets Freiligrath, Tegnér; the composers Marschner, Weber, Schumann, Liszt. The last named gave in 1841 a concert in Stettin, and called on Loewe, when he played Beethoven's F minor sonata. A very interesting anecdote is narrated in Frau Julie von Bothwell's "Lebensbilder" in connection with Liszt's visit. After the great *virtuoso* had finished the sonata, he said: "Now, Maestro, you must sing to me a ballad before I go, as I wish to take it with me." Loewe sang the old Scottish ballad, "Der Mutter Geist" (The Mother's Ghost), which his sister-in-law "Talvj" had translated

into German. Loewe had finished the wild ghostly
ballad, and Liszt was still listening in the arm-chair,
when suddenly the latter jumped up and left the room.
In the evening the concert-hall was crowded, and the
audience became impatient, for Liszt was late. Twenty
minutes after the hour announced, with downcast eyes
he entered the hall, looking like Dante in his younger
years. He played a beautiful fantasia which was not
in his programme; for Loewe's ghostly ballad had so
impressed his soul and mind, that he had to give vent
to his emotion before he could begin his solos. A storm
of applause greeted both the great *virtuoso* and Loewe,
who afterwards received Liszt's special thanks from the
platform. It is very strange to observe that neither
Liszt nor Wagner has left in writing any expression of
esteem for Loewe, though there is no doubt that both
have studied his works and profited by them. That
Wagner spoke very highly of Loewe, is proved by the
letter of Dr M. Runze (see Appendix), and by still
living artists, who testify that Wagner directed their
attention to Loewe's ballads, and recommended that
they should sing them in public.[1] In most concerts

---

[1] See also the letter from Wagner's daughter, Fräulein Eva Wagner,
printed in Appendix.

of Wagner Associations in Germany Loewe's name
appears; and Gura, one of the foremost Wagner singers,
now gives Loewe concerts. In March 1890, he gave in
the Philharmonic Society, Berlin, a Loewe evening
before a crowded audience. During the last Bayreuth
Festival he sang one evening before Frau Cosima
Wagner and her guests, in the villa "Wahnfried,"
Loewe's "Erlking" and "Heinrich der Vogler"; one of
the guests present was the daughter of Professor Sellar,
Edinburgh.

I have a great admiration for Wagner and Liszt;
still, I must confess, my admiration would be greater if
they had expressed their esteem for Loewe in writing.
Both took notice in their letters and writings of people
regarding whom the world does not care to learn anything; and knowing, as they must have done, what great
weight their recommendation would have borne in the
musical world, their neglect is less excusable.

As a vocalist Loewe achieved great triumphs in the
principal cities of Germany, as in Berlin, Dresden,
Frankfurt, Prague, and Vienna, in the last of which
he gave concerts in 1844. It was in Vienna, too,
that his friend and pupil Walther von Goethe took
him to Beethoven's grave, where Loewe pulled four

little flowers from spots beneath which Beethoven's
head, heart, right hand, and feet presumably rested,
and preserved them as cherished relics.   Professor
Fischhof introduced him at the Conservatorium to
the conductor of the Court chapel, B. Randhartinger,
with whom he had a conversation on Schubert.
Fischhof then accompanied him to Herr Streicher,
the pianoforte-manufacturer to the Imperial Court,
in whose saloon Loewe gave two concerts before an
audience consisting mainly of composers, artists, and
literary men, who received with great enthusiasm the
seven ballads he sang, including "The Bells of Spires,"
" Prinz Eugen," " The Moorish Prince," " Hochzeitlied "
(Wedding Song), and "The Erlking," of which they
particularly admired the last.   From Vienna Loewe
wrote to his wife: "I have reason to be not a little
proud of the signal effect my 'Erlking' has produced, seeing that the Vienna public have, so to speak,
grown up with Schubert's setting of the poem.   The
pleasure which the friends of art take in my compositions and singing cannot be told in words.   Yet at this
season, when the theatres are closed, all Vienna has
left town for the infinitely charming country-seats,
which one really cannot blame them for."

Being pressed to give a second concert on the 6th of April, he sang "The Erlking," the "Wedding Song," "The Pilgrim of St Just," and other ballads, amidst rapturous applause. He writes to his wife: "I lack neither fame here, nor honours, nor joy. The Viennese are splendid people, but they say in their *naïve* way, 'In summer even the Lord might give a concert, and nobody would go to it.'"

The next day the artists arranged a *soirée* in his honour, at which Dr Bacher, Herr von Puttlingen, the famous basso, Herr Staudigl, and all the musical authorities of Vienna, were present. Loewe had to open the *soirée* with "The Erlking" and the "Wedding Song," and closed it with "The Moorish Prince." He again writes to his wife: "It is as if the Viennese were spell-bound by my compositions. They listen with a breathless stillness and eagerness such as I never before experienced. I do not like to repeat here the praises they bestow upon me, nor to take them literally. For example, when they say that only now do they know what singing is, they rank me above their best singers, above their dearest Schubert! Only Beethoven, say they, they adore above all others."

In the next letter he says: "I am living here as if I

were in heaven; people here worship art and artists almost to excess; they are delightful. Herr von Vesque,
proposing my health, called me the North German
Schubert. Publishers here, however, are afraid of
the difficulties which the execution and accompaniment of my ballads offer; they call them witches'
work."

At the house of Baron Pasqualati, Loewe made the
acquaintance of the celebrated quartett-players May-
seder, Holz, Zäch, and Gross, most of whom had pur-
sued their studies under Beethoven himself. They
played one of Beethoven's quartetts, and also Loewe's
trio in G minor. Loewe was in his element. In spite
of the exertions of the preceding days, he felt himself
vigorous and gay as a youth. "I have quite fallen in
love with the Viennese, with their spirit and hearti-
ness," he says. "Spohr, in his 'Autobiography,' calls
Vienna the capital of the musical world. In Vienna
the highest standard is always applied to artistic productions, and to please there means to prove one's self
a master."

In 1847 Loewe had repeatedly the honour of singing
his ballads before her Majesty Queen Victoria, and both
the Queen and the Prince Consort evinced great interest

in his performances. The Prince Consort even turned
the leaves for Loewe with his own hand, and distinguished
him by marks of approbation.

When at Windsor, Loewe rose to the highest honours
in his profession. He happened to be for a short time
left alone in the throne-room, and being curious to
realise, not how to sing, but how to act the king, he
seated himself on the throne, where he, however, soon
forgot all about the king, and was lost in admiration of
the delightful view from the windows. But his elevated state soon came to an end when a servant entered
and politely informed him that her Majesty's secretary
wished to see him.

Besides the compositions already mentioned, Loewe
wrote several pianoforte sonatas, among them the telling " Gipsy " sonata, op. 107; further, the Sonate Elegique in F minor, very favourably criticised by R.
Schumann ; and the Sonate Brilliante in E flat, op. 41.
A trio in G minor was much praised by the Leipzig
critic, Herr Fink. Loewe also wrote a few string quartetts and duos. Miss Morgan played in 1887, at Berlin, a posthumous duo in A major with Bruno Dehn,
which was warmly received by the public. His Scottish Pictures for clarinet and pianoforte, dedicated to

his son-in-law, Major von Bothwell, are also very charming.

Loewe further composed five operas, which were performed, some in Weimar and some in Berlin, without, however, achieving a success, which is scarcely explicable, as Loewe had great dramatic talent, and was one of the most original composers, often producing the greatest effects with the simplest means, as is brilliantly proved in his ballads and oratorios. That his operas were not successful might be explained by his being occupied during forty-six years in Stettin, where he had little opportunity of studying stage effects, or of making himself familiar with the secrets of operatic representation. Those operas would certainly have become more effective had Loewe exercised his powers in the rich current of artistic life and experience as it exists in great cities like Vienna, Munich, Leipzig, Berlin, or Paris. As it was, his technical experience of the stage was limited; his imagination, however fertile, could not, with this disadvantage, enable him to realise the actual outcome of his ideals ; and it is not surprising that things turned out otherwise than as he had conceived them. He said in Vienna of himself: " In Vienna I find only confirmed what I always clearly felt

—that I ought to have from the outset entered into a wider sphere of action and larger surroundings." He, however, clung to Stettin, where the circle of his friends, and St Jacob's Church, with its grand organ, formed very strong ties. For when, in 1830, the conductorship of the orchestra of the Königstädter Theatre in Berlin was offered to him, he declined. He says: " I had found my permanent home in Stettin; nothing attracted me to leave it. A sphere of usefulness, artistic productiveness, congenial society, a circle of sympathising friends, but, above all, a happy home, and contentment at my own fireside,—all these things would never allow the wish for change to prevail in me." It will be seen that Loewe was too little of an ambitious man, but was a noble-hearted, disinterested individual, who led a patriarchal life. His wife and children, the recognition of his works by a small community, were everything for him. Unfortunately it must be said that, on the whole, Loewe was rather neglected in his own town, and did not meet with the recognition due to him; and it is astonishing that nevertheless he had the spirit to go on composing, and that even in his last works there is so much fresh and youthful life. Jean Paul very rightly says that air and admiration are the two things the artist cannot go without, and which he can and must imbibe incessantly. Without recognition there is no art.

In the revival of the interest in Loewe's works, Dr Max Runze, President of the Loewe Association, deserves the greatest credit; next to him, Frau Julie von Bothwell *née* Loewe, and A. Wellmer. Dr Runze's excellent literary contributions—'C. Loewe, eine aesthetische Beurtheilung:' Leipzig, Breitkopf & Härtel, 1884; and 'Loewe Redivivus:' Berlin, Duncker, 1888—are of intrinsic value. Frau Julie von Bothwell, eldest daughter of Loewe, an accomplished lady, has written a clever essay on "Thomas the Rhymer" (Berlin, Heimons, 1885), besides many interesting essays which have appeared in several musical periodicals, and which will soon be published in book form under the title 'Lebensbilder.' Pastor Aug. Wellmer, Stettin, has also published valuable communications regarding Loewe, especially on his oratorios ('Musikalische Skizzen und Studien:' Hildburghausen, 1884; 'Loewe, ein deutscher Tonmeister:' Leipzig, Hessischer Verlag, 1886).

Through Dr Runze's instrumentality Professor Lepsius was induced to purchase Loewe's valuable manuscripts for the Imperial Library of Berlin. Dr Runze has untiringly exerted himself on behalf of the cultivation and propagation of Loewe's works; and since the founding of the Loewe Association in Berlin in the year 1882, a number of Loewe's works, hitherto unknown, have been publicly performed. Frau Julie von Bothwell, in a most interesting letter to me, very rightly calls Runze "Der Edelste der Loeweaner."

Loewe evenings have been arranged by vocalists of note; and amongst these Eugen Gura gave Loewe evenings on the 6th and 9th December 1887 in the Berlin Singakademie, and this year in the Philharmonic Society, with extraordinary success. Two other true masters of song, Paul Bulsz and Heinrich Vogel, sang in December 1887, amidst rapturous applause, several of Loewe's ballads in the Royal Opera-house at Berlin; and the late Baron Senfft von Pilsach also spread the fame of the composer by his exquisite rendering of Loewe's ballads. Further, we must mention the talented composer, singer, and pianist, Georg Henschel, whose rendering of "Archibald Douglas" was looked upon as a pattern by reputed vocalists, and who, in a praiseworthy manner, exerted himself in England to make Loewe's ballads more generally known.

Nor must we fail to name Augustus Fricke, and the excellent baritone vocalist, Carl Mayer of Cologne, who recently sang Loewe's "Thomas the Rhymer" in London with great success.

Martin Plüddemann, a talented composer, vocalist, and music critic, whose most interesting compositions are written in the style of Loewe and Wagner; and Adolf Wallnöver, a gifted operatic singer at Prague, himself a composer of fine ballads, are also great admirers of Loewe's music, and do their best to propagate his works. Martin Plüddemann, born in Colberg in 1854, made his studies at the Leipzig Conservatoire. His ballads are published by Alfred Schmid, Munich. "Jung Siegfried," "Siegfried's Schwert," and "Der Taucher," rank with the best compositions of modern time.

Of the lady artists who have worthily represented Loewe, we have to mention Johanna Jachman Wagner, Richard Wagner's niece, Hermine Spies, and Frau A. Joachim.

There are still towns in Germany where Loewe is little known, and it must be recorded that even the people of Stettin treated him with ingratitude; for when in 1866 he had a stroke of paralysis, the municipality obliged him to resign his office. He retired to

Kiel, where he spent the last three years of his life at the house of his son-in-law, Major von Bothwell, in peaceful contemplativeness, being occasionally gratified by visits from admiring friends, among others from Johannes Brahms. The injustice of the people of Stettin he bore like a philosopher without bitterness or complaint, but he never again touched his favourite instrument the organ. It must be mentioned, however, that at present the people of Stettin are great admirers of Loewe's genius, and cultivate his works. This is largely due to the advocacy of Pastor A. Wellmer.

Loewe died on the 20th April 1869, bearing up heroically against dreadful agonies. For the organ he had a passionate fondness, and in compliance with his last wishes, his heart, so devoted to it, was buried near the organ of St Jacob's Church in Stettin, where a black marble slab marks the hallowed spot.

Not bowed down by any slight, Loewe felt his high position as a composer; he sought no greater reward than the joy of having moved and elevated human hearts.

> " He sang right as the warbler sings
>   That in the green trees liveth ;
> The song that from his full heart springs
>   Its own rich guerdon giveth."

Loewe's fame is scarcely touched by the negative
opinions of some superficial critics and pedants, who
found his compositions too difficult and eccentric, and
deviating too much from the rules of artistic tradi-
tionalism. Some of the greatest authorities, however,
—such men as Marx, Spontini, Weber, Schumann,
Mendelssohn, and R. Wagner—have recognised Loewe
as a composer of the highest genius; so that one
who has such critics in his favour may rest assured
of immortality.

" Wer den Besten seiner Zeit genug gethan
Der hat gelebt für alle Zeiten."

FRANZ SCHUBERT

G

FRANZ SCHUBERT.

FRANZ SCHUBERT was born at Vienna on the 31st of January 1797. With him came a new spring in this world,—a spring such as the world never saw before, and which will never fade away as long as any men of feeling live who shall care for and love the blossoms and flowers of art. Schubert came into this world and made mankind happier and nobler by his works; and every one who has feeling and appreciation for ideal art will remember his name with devotion and love.

Schubert is the most poetical of all musicians; he is full of charm, like Mozart—of greatness, like Beethoven.

Schubert's father was, like Loewe's, a schoolmaster who had a very small income; but he had a large family, for he was blessed with nineteen children.

How economically they had to live, how meagre was their fare, we may easily imagine. Little food and little money is the destiny of most teachers. Yet, as has so often been the case, the poor schoolmaster's humble abode proved the cradle of a musical genius.

Schubert's father was also a musician; he introduced his son into the sanctuary of his art, and strove his best to advance him in it. Of heavenly musical food there was no lack in Schubert's house, and this food has more refreshed our Franz than the most sumptuous fare could have done.

So great was the genius of Schubert, that though his life was never other than a wretched one, unvisited by prosperity, it was rendered bright and happy by an unending flow of musical thoughts.

Schubert's beautiful soprano voice and his musical ability procured him a place in the "Stadtconvikt." This institution was at that time devoted not only to science, but also to music; and the works of Haydn, Mozart, Beethoven, and Cherubini were daily studied there with care. When he was sixteen years of age, in 1813, Schubert's voice began to break, and he then left that institution. To be freed from military duties, he became, for three years, a teacher in his father's

school. It was not cowardice made him take this
step. He felt in his soul that he was chosen to far
higher things than fighting in the battle - field. In
1815 he had already written the celebrated "Ossian
Songs"; and in 1816 he wrote that well-known poetical,
melancholy song "The Wanderer," and his world-famed
"Erlking." In 1817 he wrote "Die Gruppe aus dem
Tartarus," by Schiller; "Pax Vobiscum," the words by
his friend Schober; and "Der Schiffer," the words by
his friend Meyerhofer. Between 1818 and 1824 he was
invited by Count Eszterhazy to his country seat, Zelész,
in Hungary; there he gave music lessons, and made
the acquaintance of Baron Schönstein, to whom he
dedicated his "Müllerlieder," which Schönstein sang
in such a masterly way, that even Liszt was once so
moved that tears filled his eyes. The influence of
Hungarian national music is observable in some of
Schubert's instrumental works, especially in the "Di-
vertissement à la Hongroise."

Schubert lived in Vienna in a musical and intellectual atmosphere. Besides his two friends, the nobly
cultured poet Bauernfeld and the artist (painter) M.
Schwind, Schnorr von Carolsfeld, Baron Dobelhof, and
Hofkapellmeister B. Randhartinger were his friends;

and intercourse with men so cultured must have been very beneficial to our composer. Schubert received from this society, called "Schubertiaden," a great impulse, which swayed his mind to the end of his life.

In this society Schubert was called the "Kanevas." Kreissle informs us that if any one was introduced to the society, he always asked his neighbour, "Kann er was?"—Does he know anything? Through his friend Schober he made the acquaintance of the celebrated singer M. Vogl, who sang his compositions to perfection, especially his "Winterreise" and his "Erlking."

Great interest was taken in Schubert's works by the poet Ladislaus Pyrker, Patriarch of Venice, and later Archbishop of Erlau. As a token of gratitude, Schubert dedicated to him the "Wanderer." In 1825, Schubert again met Pyrker in Gastein, whither he had gone with his friend Vogl. The sojourn was very pleasant to both, and Schubert often said that these days were the happiest of his life. There he composed some music to Walter Scott's "Lady of the Lake," the sonata in C, and his celebrated song "Die Allmacht," the words by L. Pyrker. As it is little known in this country, I may say a few words about it. This composition I would call a great tone-picture; it is a hymn of

praise, stately and full of splendour. We seem to hear
some prophet, who, with a voice of thunder, speaks to
the people of the power and the glory of the Almighty.
The greatness of God in nature is first proclaimed. The
tone-painting is full of grandeur and of majesty. Not
with the delicate, charming pencil of Fra Angelico, but
with the strong, energetic, and powerful brush of Michael
Angelo, does Schubert paint the raging of the storm, the
forest's boisterous violence, the thunder and the lightning. The painting is softer, milder, sweeter only when
he comes to the beautiful and calming words that the
power of God is high above all, and greater when man
feels it in his inmost heart, and hopes through his prayers
to be heard, and to find grace and mercy with the Most
High. Then follows a great crescendo, ending with the
powerful and mighty exclamation, "Great is Jehovah
the Lord!" which produces an overpowering effect.

..... ist Je - - ho - - - - - - - - - - - - - - - va, der Herr! etc.

etc.

Schubert would, as it were, indicate that we cannot sufficiently praise the power and the glory of the Almighty. In this composition, as scarcely in any other, Schubert, usually so charming, is very dramatic, and shows command of the loftiest expression.

In 1826 he arranged the same song for four voices, but he did not, unfortunately, quite finish it. Schubert, like Mozart, could never gain an assured position. He had to live by the honorarium that he received for his compositions, and he was, besides, unpractical, like all geniuses, and was never able to sell any of his works at a fair price. For his "Erlking" he could at first not even find a publisher, and his friends made, at a musical party, a subscription for the first hundred copies. And even after his name was better known, he did not know how to profit by his fame.

To improve his position, his friends induced him to

give a concert of his own works, which he did on the
6th of March 1827. Besides a new trio and quartett,
several new songs were then given; and at this concert
" Die Allmacht" was first performed by Vogl.

Every piece, says Bauernfeld, was warmly received,
and the composer was several times recalled. The
concert brought him 800 gulden—just as much as
twelve volumes of his songs had done. This great success made Schubert quite happy. It was to be, alas!
the last glimpse of light on his thorny path of life.
His friends purposed to give two other Schubert concerts, but they were only given to pay the expenses of
his burial.

Schubert has, for his short life, like Mozart, given to
the world quite an incomprehensible wealth of music.
The poems of the greatest German poet specially inspired him—and so for the song a new epoch began
with Schubert, in whose hands the melody and the
piano accompaniment together reveal the mysteries,
and delineate the inmost feelings, of the human
heart.

Schubert's importance in the history of music is in
perfect analogy with the importance of Goethe as a
lyric poet in the history of poetry. One hundred songs

of Goethe were set to music by Schubert, but other
poets, too, have inspired him; there is hardly a poet
to whom he has not given a melodious sign of love as
he passed on his way. His stream of song was like
the spring which flows from a rock, inexhaustible and
pure. In the short space of seventeen years Schubert
wrote six operas, eight symphonies, several masses,
sonatas, quartetts, trios, polonaises, and six hundred
songs. "If productiveness," says Schumann, the enthusiastic admirer of Schubert, "is the first sign of a
genius, then Schubert is one of the greatest." It is
indisputable that Schubert is the greatest of song-
writers; he is the king of song. The songs of Schubert indicate, like the ballads of Loewe, the operas
of Mozart, the symphonies of Beethoven, the perfection of modern classical art. Schubert lived near
Beethoven. As in their lives, so in their work,—
Beethoven and Schubert are never far from one
another.

Schindler, in his biography of Beethoven, says that
Beethoven only made the acquaintance of Schubert's
works towards the very end of his life. The great composer was surprised to see so many songs, and still more
so after he had read them. He could not but speak in

admiration of Schubert's genius, and daily he studied
for hours such as the " Müllerlieder," " Die junge
Nonne," "Die Grenzen der Menschheit," and "Die
Allmacht." Enthusiastically he exclaimed, " Verily,
verily, in Schubert there lives a divine spark ! "

As my readers are probably already familiar with
Schubert's biography, I propose merely to add to it a
few anecdotes which I have myself heard from the
venerable Herr Benedikt Randhartinger.

B. Randhartinger was born in 1802, at Ruprechtsho-
fen, Austria, and is now in his eighty-ninth year. Himself a talented composer of sacred music and songs, he
was a schoolfellow of Schubert at the Stadtconvikt,
Vienna, where they both studied harmony and counterpoint under Salieri. Randhartinger was for ten years
secretary to Count Szécsényi, and in 1832 he entered as
a tenor in the Court chapel. In 1862 he became conductor of the Court chapel. He has written twenty
masses, two symphonies, and several works of chamber
music, with a great many songs, some in the early style
of Schubert. He also wrote one opera, " Enzio," but
without success. He is one of the few surviving Germans who had the privilege of knowing Beethoven,
and was one of the most intimate friends of Schubert.

Four years ago, when I spent my summer holidays at Gloggnitz (Austria), near the snow mountain, I made the acquaintance of the amiable old gentleman, who at that time was on a visit to his son-in-law, Herr Friedrich Ehrbar, pianoforte-manufacturer to the Court. At Herr Ehrbar's house we met nearly every day, and always devoted an hour or two to music. I sang mostly songs and ballads by Schubert and Loewe, and the kindly old gentleman was the first to urge me to sing in public the ballads of Loewe by way of comparison with those of Schubert. In spite of his great admiration of and friendship for Schubert, he at once acknowledged the genius of Loewe, spoke with great enthusiasm about his ballads and his singing, and could even name all the ballads which he had heard in 1844, when Loewe first gave his concerts in Vienna. Herr Randhartinger remarked that although Loewe's ballads are more dramatic, he liked Schubert's better, as they are more *cantabile* in style. I had very often to sing to him Schubert's " Die Allmacht," " Die Gruppe aus dem Tartarus," and Loewe's " Oluf," " Erlking," and " Odins Meeresritt," and he always encouraged me with his approbation, and as a reward sang to me some of his own charming compositions. I must con-

fess that the singing of the old gentleman of eighty-
four moved me more than the singing of the first tenor
in the Court Opera. After the music, Herr Randhartinger was very communicative, and related many
interesting anecdotes about Schubert. He told me, for
example, how the celebrated "Müllerlieder" came to
be composed. When Randhartinger resided in the
Herrengasse, Vienna, Schubert often called and invited
him to take a walk. On one occasion Schubert saw
on Randhartinger's table a book by W. Müller containing the so-called "Müllerlieder": he read some
of these poems, and without awaiting Randhartinger's
return, he took away the book about five o'clock in the
afternoon, and went straight home to compose. When
Randhartinger returned, he looked in vain for the
book, as he had also intended to set some of Müller's
poems to music. Next forenoon he called at Schubert's lodging, and was surprised to see the book on
Schubert's table. "Do not be angry with me, dear
Benedictus" (so he called Randhartinger); "the poems
have so inspired me that I had to compose music to
them, and I scarcely slept two hours last night, and
now you see the result. I have already seven poems
set to music. I hope you will like my songs; will you

try them ?" Randhartinger at once sang the first seven songs. He was delighted, and said: "I will never touch the book again; keep it, as, after Schubert, Benedictus has no right to compose." In the course of one week the whole series of the "Müllerlieder" were composed, and I believe never before were poetry and music more lovingly united than in these songs.

Among many other interesting anecdotes of Schubert I may select two. Schubert, poor man, was always short of money, though not always through his own fault. He once called on Randhartinger and asked him for the loan of 15 florins to pay the rent of his lodgings, in order to avoid being turned out. Randhartinger at once gave him the necessary sum, and they both went to the proprietor and paid the 15 florins. As they passed the "Graben," the street where the music publisher Diabelli had his shop, Schubert said: "Dear Benedictus, I would repay you at once if these people here could pay me for my songs; they have a great many of my compositions, but every time I ask for money they always say they had too much outlay and too little income from my songs. I called twelve times at Diabelli's, but I have not yet received one

penny; but I shall never give them a song again."
He sold Diabelli the copyright of twelve volumes of
his songs for 800 florins (£70); while on one single
song, the "Wanderer," Diabelli is said to have made a
profit of no less than 36,000 florins (£3000).

In Schubert's Biography the Court opera-singer Vogl
is always mentioned as having been the first to sing the
"Erlking" in public. Randhartinger, however, told
me the following facts: "I was still at school in the
'Stadtconvikt' of Vienna, when one day Schubert,
who was quite excited, brought me the manuscript of
the 'Erlking,' and asked me, then a boy of fourteen,
to sing it. Like lightning the news flashed through
the institution that Franzl (so they called Schubert)
was there, and had brought a new composition. In a
trice the concert-room of the institution was filled with
the students and teachers, and Randhartinger was
chosen to sing for the first time Schubert's grand
composition, accompanied by the young composer himself. The beautiful playing of Schubert, and the spir-
ited singing of Randhartinger, inspired the whole audience, and the 'Erlking' had to be repeated. Schubert,
who was very modest, said: 'Benedictus, the song pleases
me too, if only it were not so very difficult to play.'

The second time Schubert omitted the triplets, and replaced them by quavers. Some of the teachers asked him why he omitted the triplets. Schubert replied, 'They are too difficult for me; a *virtuoso* may play them.' The second time Randhartinger sang with more expression and animation, and there followed quite a storm of applause. 'Of all good things there are three!' shouted the students, and poor Schubert and Randhartinger had to perform the 'Erlking' for the third time." Never, probably, has the "Erlking" been heard in such perfection. In both the young artists the sacred fire was burning, while young and old imagined themselves transported to fairyland.

The honorarium for this and other performances consisted, apart from enthusiasm, in presents of music-paper, which the students gave Schubert that he might be able to compose more.

The manuscript which Randhartinger received from Schubert is now in the possession of Frau Clara Schumann, whose husband was not only a great admirer of Schubert's genius, but has, next to Liszt, done most for the propagation of his works.

It was very noble in Randhartinger to part with that

valuable manuscript; but old Randhartinger is ever
young in imagination, and at command everything
appears fresh before his eyes—the memorable day in
the year 1816, victorious Schubert, the crowded hall,
and the inspired audience.

LOEWE'S BALLADS

LOEWE'S BALLADS.

In composing his Art ballads, or dramas in miniature, as I have called them, Loewe struck out a new
course, and suggested the present music-drama, as
created by Richard Wagner. The principles which
Wagner laid down in his philosophical and æsthetic
dissertations on "the Art of the future" in 1851,
Loewe had actually carried out thirty years before in
his earliest works, "Erlking," "Oluf," and "Edward."
In these compositions it was not Loewe's sole object to
write charming melody, but to find for the subject and
its respective elements the truest and most adequate
musical expression. He possessed the capacity of entering thoroughly into the spirit of the poetry, and was
therefore not merely a composer, but also a poet. His

melodies seem to spring from the poetry, and are the embodiment of its spirit. "The verse-melody," says Richard Wagner, "is the explanatory link between the language of words and that of musical sound, the off-spring of the union of poetry with music, the most supreme union of both arts." Loewe, with the instinct of genius, found it absolutely necessary to individualise the *dramatis personæ*, the scenes, and the local peculiarities of the mythical poems, which he set to music by means of certain motives through which he clearly differentiated them. And he thus created the method of the so-called *Leitmotive*, and applied to the ballad the system which Richard Wagner has broadly and ex-haustively carried out in his dramas or giant ballads, "The Flying Dutchman," "Lohengrin," "Tannhäuser," "Nibelungen."

The recognition of this as the appropriate style for the composition of the ballad, comprising, as it does, so many different elements, entitles Loewe to rank with the outstanding genius of Wagner, and makes him the forerunner and pioneer of all contemporary and subse-quent masters who have written ballads and dramatic oratorios. Loewe was and is still carefully studied, imitated, and exploited by many composers, but often without acknowledgment. His compositions are not readily appreciated, being too difficult, too much off the beaten track, and too far divergent from the old traditions, so that they can never attain to great popularity in the ordinary sense. We know by experience that only such works as are within reach of the intellect of the majority meet with a ready reception and instant popularity. Wagner's " Flying Dutchman," for instance, was performed in Vienna—the musical capital of the world—twenty years after its creation; and in many musical towns Wagner's works were only introduced thirty years after their publication. Loewe's greatness is only now being recognised; and the better acquainted we are with his works, the more we will like and cultivate him: hence it is for the future to acknowledge Loewe in his entirety. If we look over the great number of books containing Loewe's ballads, we are astonished at the new, quite original spiritual world which opens before us, at the abounding wealth of ideas and forms. I would call Loewe a magician, who only needed to touch with his wand the strangest poetry, and called forth the most fantastic creations; nay, it might well be that he was not only intimate with the spirits of the vasty deep, but had entered into a compact with

them, forcing them to assist him. For the power of
production, the freshness, the unfading youthfulness
and diversity found in his works are marvellous, and
wellnigh boundless.   O. Gumprecht says : " His is that
fantastic fairy world which has ever irresistibly attracted man's senses into its mysterious domains.   The
tales of all times and peoples have given the composer
material for his works.   We see him dig indefatigably
in the remotest mines of the myth.   The call of his
voice was heard by the most cunning spirits and the
most horrible demons with whom poetry peoples air,
water, caves, and precipices.   Equally marvellous is
Loewe's productiveness and the diversity found in his
works.   What an endless bewitching series of colours
and forms !   We see gay Greek gods singing and playing ;
scenes from the Bible, Christian saints and martyrs
pass before us.   The poetic traditions of the northern
mythology living in the depths of the people's soul, all
the characteristic types of the middle ages, Brahmans
Turks, Moors, erotic figures of every stamp—a veritable
orbis pictus in tone is given to us in Loewe's works.
His imagination was at home in all regions; it races
with the storm and with the cloud over the northern
heather, and it revels entranced in the glowing colours

and beauties of the south." The musical motives, in-
vented and developed in the most masterly way by
Loewe, are, without exception, interesting and original,
both in melody, harmony, and rhythm. He allowed
nothing but the intention of the poet to influence him
in his choice of means of expression, and whenever
the dramatic or tragic situation demanded special accentuation, he did not hesitate to introduce harsh, unprepared modulations and dissonances, exploring, nay,
even expanding the means of musical expression. Narrow - minded, antiquated theorists and critics of his
time declared such daring constructions to be eccentric,
forbidding, and belonging at best to the category of
"the music of the future," a thing to be shunned and
proscribed.

Where such passages occur in Loewe's works, however, they are by no means forced or far-fetched with
a view to show originality, but they always seem to
spring up spontaneously as the natural outcome of a
forcible idea seeking its appropriate realistic expression.
Daring progressions and modulations, discords based on
an intentionally long delay in resolving the suspended
notes, the repeated accentuation of a dissonant interval,
and other such effects, are only used whenever the ballad,

with its tendency towards the supernatural, calls for a
mystic tone-colour and unfamiliar form. And in this
branch of the art, no composers have yet so well understood as Loewe and Wagner how to make music thoroughly subserve their theme. From all this we may
gather that the instrumental part—*i.e.*, the accompaniment—in Loewe's ballads is an important factor, and is
generally conceived in a polyphonic, orchestral style.[1]

"THE FISHERMAN" (*Goethe*).

To Goethe, the friend of nature, it was not only a
heavenly enjoyment to rove through fields and woods,
but it was also his irresistible desire to allow the cool
waves of water and air to surround him. Whoever
knows the beautiful valley of the Ilm, and the lovely
banks of the Saale, will recognise that Goethe has so
loved the naiads of those streams, as to portray their
features when writing on the spirits and gods of flood
and water. We can scarcely read Goethe's poem
" The Fisherman," without thinking of the charming
Ilm, which has its course very near to Goethe's

---

[1] Some of Loewe's ballads ("Night Parade," "Walpurgis Nacht," and
others) are also written and published for orchestra.

garden-house in Weimar, and in which on quiet moonlight summer nights Goethe, then an "Apollo with the
strength of an athlete," was accustomed to dive into
the flood. Like Goethe, Loewe and Schubert felt the
sincerest admiration for nature, and were inspired by
the beauty of Goethe's poem to set it to music. In
Goethe's "Fisherman" the witchery of the world of
waters has been realised in an enchanting way; it
belongs, like the "Erlking," to Goethe's most popular
ballads. It shows us the treacherous element reflect-
ing on its smooth surface the firmament, with the stars
and our own face, and still for ever tearing from light
and life the imprudent one who without resistance
allows himself to be drawn into "the eternal dew"
—a symbol of sensual love, which betrays him who
yields to its allurements and forfeits his soul. Some
see in it the power of attraction of the Unknown, the
Infinite, which draws man into its mysterious depths.
All this and still more is contained in this ballad—for
every really great work comprises a mysterious something not to be analysed, which makes itself known
to our senses, but which love alone can understand
in its full grandeur. We see in this ballad how nymphs
and elves—those spirits of *modern* mythology—have as

great a charm for us as those of the old world; they
are not dead, as is believed in this material world of
ours; a great poet need only conjure them up, and they
will appear in undying glory. Schubert has treated
Goethe's "Fisherman," as mentioned before, like a song,
giving it even as such a very primitive form. He
characterises the motion of the water by a little figure
of semiquavers, carried out in the accompaniment
throughout, but there is only *one* tune used for all
the verses. The major mode gives it a pleasing, tranquil character; moreover, there are no other modulations in it, except the common one to the dominant and
subdominant, the relative minor being avoided. It
belongs to the category of a strophic song, based on the
simplest principle of song-form, consisting of a double
period, each of which contains eight bars. The changing scenes of the ballad Schubert has totally ignored
—the mystic mood, the longing of the nymph, the
succumbing of the lad, the tragic accents of the words,
"and ne'er again was seen," are not expressed in the
least in his setting. What we hear is a charming
song, leaving a pleasant impression behind, like
everything Schubert's music produced, but no ballad.
Loewe's "Fisherman" (in E major) offers a striking con-

trast to all we have had to say about Schubert's: it
is a ballad—it characterises, it unfolds rich means of
illustration, it consists of several divisions, each dealing with one verse. The prelude and first narrative
parts express in a splendid fashion the predominant
mood. The accompaniment contains a very descriptive restless figure, indicating the rise and fall of the
waves. The song of the water-nymph brings a modulation into the key of the subdominant, A natural;
and the accompaniment to its sweet alluring melody
is somewhat less impassioned, though containing semiquavers which, however, instead of moving in unequal
intervals, smoothly pass on in broken chords; half
mourning, half caressing is the nymph's chant, which
develops into a fine cantilene. The tenor part of the
accompaniment brings in a beautiful motive—

Tenero e dolce.

which alternately precedes and succeeds, or interferes
with, the phrases which appear in the vocal part,
and hence the lovely passages resemble a duet. The
greatest crescendo and climax of feeling is reached in
the tones which Loewe found for the words—

"The deep, deep heavens then lure thee not?"

Lockt dich ... der tie · · · · · fe Him · · · · mel.

Such heartfelt strains we find rivalled only in Wagner's works. The nymph's alluring words are finely expressed in her concluding verse, in which part of the melodious strain, formerly appearing in A, is now transposed into E natural, and is carried out in a rich development, modulating into C sharp minor. The lad's final yielding to the nymph's entreaty is rendered by a fine crescendo—

"Half drew she him, and half he sank."

Halb zog · sie · · ·

mf

ihn, · · · · halb · · · · sank · · er · · · · · · · · · · ·

f

The postlude refers to the motives of the introduction, bringing in a reminiscence of the figure which
previously accompanied the strains of the water-
nymph ; it is also transposed into E, and somewhat
abbreviated.

In Loewe's setting, Goethe's " Fisherman " has indeed
become a dramatic event—the two arts, music and
poetry, being wedded in it so as to form one.

"THE ERLKING" (*Goethe*).

" The Erlking " is no doubt Goethe's most popular
ballad, and it may be of some interest to say a few words
about its origin. It was an insignificant incident which
impelled Goethe to create this wonderful poem. He was
of course acquainted with Herder's translation of the
Danish ballad " Sir Oluf," which tells us how that
knight, on his way to the wedding-feast, meets the
Erlking's daughter, and comes by his death. More than
the mention of the Erlking's daughter and the death-

bringing air of the wood we do not, however, find in Goethe's poem. The story is, that one autumn night Goethe was walking to and fro in his little garden, when a rider passed the gate at full gallop. The nocturnal rider made a deep impression on the poet's mind. He inquired about him, and learned it was a farmer with his sick boy in his arms, hastening to see a doctor at Jena. This gave the impulse, and a wonderful poem was created, in which the most consummate work of art is combined with the simplicity of national song. The emotions of three distinct persons are represented ascending to the highest pathos. The poem is at the same time as short as possible. With the swiftness of an arrow it passes on, rising and falling, and resembling in its rhythm the galloping of a horse. The dramatic treatment of the incident discloses at once the minutest details of the landscape—night, fog, storm, withered leaves, venerable willows, long vistas which open before our eyes, showing us the Erlking, with his crown and long robe of mist, reigning in his empire, and approaching to frighten the poor child to death. It is interesting to note that both Loewe and Schubert published the "Erlking" as op. 1, and both in G minor.

A letter from Frau Julie von Bothwell informed me

that her father had seen the manuscript of Schubert's
"Erlking" previous to his setting the same ballad to
music. Although it was against his principle to set
to music poems which were composed before him by
other masters, Loewe felt that Schubert had not found
the true ballad-tone for this poem, and therefore he
wrote the music to it in a more dramatic style, saying,
"*Man kann es auch anders machen*"—"It can be done
in another way."

Loewe's "Erlking," as we have said, is written in
G minor, and a mysterious mood predominates. The
prelude and first part describe the motion of the ride
in strongly marked accents and great hasty strides.
The two voices of father and son are distinguished from
one another in point of melody, and later on they are
contrasted rhythmically and dynamically — the son
speaks high and excitedly, the father quietly and low.
To the fundamental mood, the lyrical part of this
ballad—that is, the singing of the Erlking—forms a
complete contrast. Loewe chose the tonic major (G)
for this second subject, and allows the melodic phrase,
of eight bars, to be based entirely on the harmony of
the common chord without the aid of any modulation.
This strange proceeding lends to the repeated appear-

I

ance of this phrase a magic power, which entrances
and ensnares us until we fully understand the awe of
the child.

Komm lie - - - bes   Kind   Komm - geh'   mit   mir,   gar.

It is clear that it was Loewe's intention to give the
Erlking's voice a monotonous mystic character, and
hence to abstain from modulations, which he, the
melodious and inexhaustible in invention, would not
have been at a loss to find here, as everywhere else.
His conception seems to me more to the point than
that of Schubert, who allows the Erlking to address
the boy in tones so caressing and sweet, that we scarcely
understand how they could have alarmed him. Loewe's
voice of the Erlking fascinates, intrudes, forces, and
the boy succumbs to the magic spell at once; Schubert's
Erlking allures the child in loving, human, and realistic
tones. Loewe has thus found the more characteristic
way of expressing the whispering of the misty spectre,
and has given the whole ballad the right balance. The
accompaniment to the Erlking's melody consists of a
uniform tremolo between the major third and the fifth
of G—

which, supported in the bass by the full chord, contributes materially to give the melody something of an impetuous, dominating character. A new motive appears in the accompaniment before the first repetition of the Erlking's lyric phrase, and distinctly illustrates the spell, into which the child is gradually sinking.

This motive has a striking likeness to one in Wagner's "Ride of the Walkyries," and it was very interesting for me to observe the impression which this ballad, with its grand finale, made upon my esteemed friend Sarasate. I sang it to him without mentioning the name of the composer, and he exclaimed enthusiastically, "*É molto bello, mi pare é qualche cosa di Wagner*"—"This is very beautiful, and seems to be something by Wagner." Towards the end the above

motive is dealing heavy blows; the magic power becomes stronger and mightier; the alluring melody is
succeeded by a grand *ensemble*. The child's and the
father's fears are boundless; the spell follows hard after
them; the horse gallops with breathless speed through
the lonely forest. Loewe here modulates with strong
colours from G minor into E flat minor, then into B natural
and G major, four mediant modulations in one breath,
until, by means of the seventh on C and the chord of
the augmented sixth on E flat, he reaches G minor.

The final words "the child was dead," Loewe, like

Schubert, composed in the recitative form, delaying,
however, the cadence by striking the dissonant note B
natural, and leaving it to the accompaniment to bring
the ballad to a full close. The last four bars, based on
an organ-point (G) in the bass, form a worthy cadence to
this sublime tone-picture. Loewe's "Erlking" gives the
vocalist rather a difficult task as to compass and execution; a soft flexible voice is also required to do full
justice to the lyrical phrases, and in the more excited
parts the vocalist must possess considerable power of
dramatic expression, and be master of the declamatory
style of singing. Loewe's "Erlking" would be just
as popular as that by Schubert, were it not for
the great demands it makes upon the singer. For
its artistic representation, a strict characterisation of
the different persons is indispensable, and for this
end one must necessarily have a mastery of vocal
colours. The father requires a dark timbre, the son
a clear one, the Erlking a semi-dark, mystic timbre;
moreover, the vocalist must have full command over his
voice, in order to be able to produce all degrees, from
piano to forte and fortissimo. The last words must be
more declaimed than sung; only I would advise
vocalists not to make too long a pause before the word
"todt" (dead), as indicated in the music, for too literal

a rendering of the rests would, in my opinion, annihilate
the dramatic effect. I would also suggest the following
change in the vocal part to baritones with limited
compass:—

ORIGINAL VERSION.

Gewalt!" mein Va-ter mein Va-ter jetzt fasst er mich an, Erl-kö-nig

hat mir ein Leids ge-than, Erl-kö-nig hat mir ein Leids ge-than.

PROPOSED ALTERATION.

Gewalt!" mein Va-ter mein Va-ter jetzt fasst er mich an, Erl-kö-nig

hat mir ein Leids ge-than, Erl-kö-nig hat mir ein Leids ge-than.

The alterations shown above do not harm the
character of the composition, as this phrase does not
possess any special melodic importance, and a very
rich accompaniment in any case nearly drowns the
singing voice. Although I am, as a rule, against
changing anything in classical works, I consider the
suggested alteration necessary, in order to make the
ballad attainable to more vocalists, and thus help it to
gain greater popularity. Richard Wagner once said to

his pupils: " My young friends, you think Schubert's
' Erlking' to be the best.   Listen! here is one much
finer; it is that by Loewe.   Schubert's ' Erlking' is not
quite true, but Loewe's is true."

"THE FLOWER'S REVENGE" (*Freiligrath*).

This is one of the longest and most fascinating works
written by Loewe in ballad form; descriptive and lyric
elements predominate in it.   The poem calls for diversified, illustrative treatment, and for frequent change
in tone and colour.   The ballad consists of five short
divisions, each of which contains new subjects; the
concluding verses reproduce the thematic material of
the first division, but, in accordance with the demands of the poem, with somewhat different treatment and arrangement.   The ballad begins with a
simple melody in A minor ($\frac{6}{8}$), accompanied by
chords, and developed in a tranquil unpretending
fashion, modulating into F major, and bringing in as
a second subject a very undulatory motive in the vocal
part.   This consists of a quaver, followed by two semi-
quaver triplets, portraying the many-folded garlands of
roses, and flowers of every description, which are confined within a vase beside the slumbering maiden's bed.

A very flexible voice is required for the execution of these pretty figures,

Schim · · · · mernd auf . . . dem   Bin · · · · sen · · stuh · le.

which are intended by the composer to be sung in a soft and dreamy manner.   In the next part ($\frac{4}{8}$ *allegro*) the triplet figure is given to the accompaniment, but in another form ; the passing notes are mostly chromatic, and there are pauses after each appearance of the little motive :—

The intervals of the vocal part contain a broken, ascending, chromatic scale, frequently interrupted by pauses.   The singer has to use a minimum of tone for these verses, so as not to drown the pretty figures in the accompaniment, which, though piano, still distinctly follow the flower-spirits' busy movements.

Plötz-lich, horch !   Plötz-lich, horch !

The instrumental as well as the vocal parts become more and more vivid and pressing when a *molto mo- derato fantastico* $\frac{3}{4}$ appears, changing the whole scene.

The poetic verses, telling of a "gentle fair one" rising from the rose's flowery cup, call forth a beautiful melodious strain, which, based on A minor, modulates into C major and A flat minor. It is one of Loewe's lyric pearls. A pretty contrast is offered by the succeeding *piu animato*, in which is represented the negro's coming forth from a Turkish turban (*Lilium martagon*), and a veritable Turkish march whirls on before us. The triplet figures reappear in the description of the flowers coming nearer the maiden's bed, dancing and swaying around her. The second lyric passage—the flowers' complaint, as it might be called (*dolce, moderato, con pieta,* 𝄌), prepared by a little *intermezzo* (*con dolore*) —reminds us of the Rhine-daughters, in Wagner's "Siegfried," mourning for their lost gold, which gave them lustre and light in the depths of the flood. The flowers sing: "Maiden, maiden, from the earth thou cruelly hast torn us; we now must fade and wither, in a coloured crystal vase."

Dolce, moderato, con pieta.

Mäd - chen, Mäd - chen! aus der
Er - - - de hast du grau - - - - - sam uns geris - sen.

The melody is of an enchanting sweetness and simplicity, and takes a very expressive turn at the words, "Clear dew and rain surrounded us once; now in a filthy water we lie!"

Einst . . . . um - floss   uns,   Thau . . . . und Re - - gen.

The flower - spirits creep nearer the maiden; they constantly whisper and murmur, breathing revenge and death. In the accompaniment now appears the triplet-motive in this arrangement—

The F major subject from the first part reappears, leading to the cadential phrases, which give an adequate expression to the idea that the maiden's slumber has become an eternal sleep: the flowers' revenge is accomplished! A languid lassitude is represented by the concluding bars of this poetic composition.

"The Night Parade" (*Zedlitz*).

This belongs to the cabinet pieces among Loewe's ballads; in it we most distinctly recognise his power of tone-painting. Baron von Schönstein, to whom Schubert dedicated his celebrated "Müllerlieder," writes of Schubert that he carried with him the poem "The Night Parade" for many weeks, for the author had expressed a wish that he should set it to music. At last Schubert returned the book, modestly confessing himself not inclined to the work, being afraid he would not be able to write good music for it. Felix Mendelssohn, too, was asked by Frau Pereira, in Vienna, to set it, but he also refused, declaring that narrative poetry was not suitable for setting to music (Mendelssohn's 'Letters,' vol. i.) Loewe, however, was immensely taken by this ballad, and at once found the right tone for it. He discovered marvellous means of expression for its dismal gloomy character—tone-effects such as had scarcely been surpassed. First of all, the softly vibrating drum-effect opening the prelude of the immensely pathetic first part, which stands, in respect of tone-colour, above everything previously written in this form.

The drum-motive is carried out, in the accompaniment throughout the first part, in G minor, which pro-
ceeds in the rhythm of a funeral march, measured and
slow.   The vocal part is to be interpreted in a declamatory style; it lends to the march, which is carried on in
the instrumental part, a melancholy melody, in a somewhat low register, so as to allow the drum-motives to
be distinctly heard.   In the course of the narration the
theme becomes more animated, and strange elements
associate themselves with it, recalling to our mind the
soldiers lying in the soil of the north, and those in
Italy, and telling us of their approach at midnight on
their flying horses.   Here occurs an opportunity for a
contrasting theme, which Loewe has not overlooked.
He introduces new means of expression, leaving the
original key and modulating by chromatic progressions
into B flat major, the relative of G minor: the ghosts
are, so to speak, gaining flesh and blood, the battle-field
on which the great Napoleon fought is becoming popu-

lated. Loewe here starts a beautiful theme, which again bears the character of a march, but of quite a different style. The major mode, the richer harmonisation, the energetic bright melody, stamp it as the more realistic tune of enthusiastic soldiers. This melody is based on a French national song, which well suits the occasion. The whole theme is carried on with great *verve*, and culminates in a bright *ensemble* at the words, " with song and sound the whole army passes by." A beautiful little phrase interrupts this march; it represents the appearance of the general, " Napoleon, with his simple hat and dress," with tender touching tones, which form a contrast with the former and the following parts. The loud music of the troops passing before him is soon silenced, while the general gives the soldiers nearest him a single word. Like the splash of death the passwords " France " and " Sanct Helena " resound through the ranks; the clear notes of the common chord of D, given to the words " Sanct Helena," are answered by the same motive in the bass, sounding like a mysterious echo, and reminding us involuntarily of the celebrated beat of the kettle-drum in Beethoven's IX. Symphony.

The drummer beats his drum again, as at the beginning; the battle-field is again empty; the troops are retiring into their graves. The march-motives of the prelude set in, and one part in the accompaniment sustains the dominant note D: it is like a gloomy complaint arising from the depths of the earth, and the drum, with abrupt rolls, beats the time to it.

I believe that Schumann, in writing his composition "Die beiden Grenadiere" to words by Heine, did so under the influence of this ballad. He introduces, as is well known, the "Marseillaise" in that composition; and Wagner, who set the same ballad to music during his sojourn in Paris (about 1840), has likewise introduced the "Marseillaise" in it, but, curiously enough,

he used German words after a French translation of
Heine's poem.

"Sir Oluf" (*Herder*).

This northern myth, full of dramatic interest, afforded
Loewe an opportunity of introducing a greater range of
variety into his *Leitmotives* than in the preceding
ghost-ballad. The acting persons—Oluf, his mother,
his bride, the elf — are here introduced conversing;
hence there are, besides the narrative parts, four indi-
viduals to be distinctively represented. The fine introduction, describing Oluf's ride, is an *allegro vivace*
($\frac{4}{4}$) in E minor, with determined accents *fortissimo*.
A charming tripping dance-motive, strangely coloured
by the interesting harmonisations, announces the presence of the elf's domains.

These motives reappear as accompaniment to the
vocal phrases: they form a very pretty effect when in
combination with the elf's song, which introduces a

half-mocking, half-seducing melody, based on the intervals of the chord of the seventh on the tonic of E minor.

Will - kom - men Herr O - - luf komm tan - ze   mit mir.

Sir Oluf resists the elf with manly, energetic accents,
emphasised by rich chords in the accompaniment.   The
dance-motive and the elf's songs are varied in accordance with the words, and a particularly charming passage occurs where the elf tells Oluf how her mother
bleaches the gauzy garments in the moonlight: the
accompaniment is figured, and stands an octave higher
than the preceding phrases, producing a bewitching
tone-effect.   A great uproar in all parts follows the elf's
"dealing Oluf a blow on the heart"; this is marked by
strong discordant accents.   Oluf's ride - motives reappear, and he is hunted out of the elf's empire with
double force.   The instrumental part illustrates Oluf's
flight by a long *coda*, at the end of which the galloping
sounds die away, and key and mood are changed.   In
the scene following, Oluf's mother welcomes her son,
asking him "Why he is so pale?"   The accompaniment, with chords alternately belonging to E major and
to C ♯ minor, indicates, by the quaver-pause which occurs

after each second and fourth beat, something anxious
and inquisitive; while Oluf answers with a stern, solemn
phrase, which recalls the elf-motives in E minor, but
altered, slow, and wearied. A charming contrast is
afforded by the following *andantino* in E major ($\frac{2}{4}$),
which is based on a plain rural melody, suggesting the
wedding-feast preparing in Oluf's house. The simple
harmonisation, resembling hunting-horn sounds, well
illustrates the pastoral scene.

A deep shadow is thrown over the final phrases given
in recitative form by the change into the minor mode,
and by the gloomy motives which, though altered in form
and rhythm, distinctly recall the elf's spell. During
the eight last bars all parts of the score are written in
unison, and in a low position. The last scene is a fine
example of musical declamation. The chord of E minor,
struck *fortissimo*, brings this highly dramatic ballad to
a close.

Spontini, on first hearing this ballad, called it a great

tragedy, and tears rolled down his cheeks. Prince Anton Radziwill[1] wrote to Loewe : "After having heard 'Sir Oluf' sung by you, I have pointed out you, dear director, as the only musician predestined to write the music to Goethe's 'Faust.'" Wagner is reported to have said regarding this ballad, that it is one of the most important works which musical literature possesses.

"HEROD'S LAMENT FOR MARIAMNE" (*Byron*).

Loewe was deeply distressed by the death of his beloved wife Julie, and in that sad state of mind he set to music Byron's Hebrew Melodies, of which "Herod's Lament for Mariamne" is a real masterpiece : we can scarcely hear it without being moved. "Herod's Lament," like the other Hebrew melodies, was a great favourite of Felix Mendelssohn, whose sister Fanny used to say that these compositions of Loewe's always lay on his piano. "I had to prevent his setting to music these poems of Byron, as Loewe's music to them is already so

---

[1] Radziwill himself devoted several years of hard work to setting Goethe's 'Faust' to music, and it is still performed every year in memory of the prince in the Berlin Singakademie.

sublime; and brother Felix has obeyed." In 1826, at
the house of Marx, Loewe made the personal acquaintance of Mendelssohn; in the following year Loewe
arranged a concert for him in Stettin, when the two
composers played a double *concerto*, which was received
with great enthusiasm. The next day Mendelssohn
called at Loewe's house, and persuaded him to sing
" Herod's Lament." Loewe complied, and the piece
made such a deep impression upon Mendelssohn that he
could not forget it for years afterwards. The music to
the pathetic verses of that grand poem ranks with the
best Loewe has written. It is a composition in which
melodic charm, genuine pathos, and fine thematic work
are combined as we only find them in classical works
of the highest order. A dramatic agitated mood pre-
vails, for the verses speak in powerful accents of King
Herod's grief for his spouse, Marianne, whose death
he had himself caused. Lyric phrases, generally the
characteristic feature of song, only occur in the second
part of this composition, which, on account of the
predominating, passionate, tragic character, ranks between the aria and the song. It is a species called in
German *Gesang* instead of *Lied* (song), the latter being
considered to have smaller dimensions than the former.

The plaintive chant is written in F minor (*allegro, assai agitato,* $\frac{4}{4}$), and introduced by an interesting phrase appearing in the prelude, and fully developed in the passages following:—

The vocal part first moves on in broad lines, whilst the counterpart of this subject has a more vigorous rhythm and melody, based on the following motives—

the accentuated notes of which also appear in the vocal part, giving these phrases special emphasis. It is the proper musical rendering of the two emotions conflicting with each other in Herod's breast—grief and passionate repentance. The motives are, later on, carried out in semiquavers instead of in triplets, and in contrary motion, thus contributing to realise a powerful *crescendo*, inspired by the words of the poem.

Ich sehe nun das . . . . sel . . . . . be

Schwert mir dro . . . . hend blit - zen.

etc.

The second subject is prepared for by a transition part, which introduces some extraneous modulations, landing in B minor. A beautiful, sweet, melodious lament in B minor, modulating into G major, and accompanied by motives of the first subject, but in modified treatment, now introduces the sentimental verse :—

" She's gone, who shared my diadem ;
    She sunk, with her my joys entombing ;
I swept that flower from Judah's stem,
    Whose leaves for me alone were blooming."

The accompaniment to this middle part is particularly
fine, often producing the effect of a violin *obligato*
supporting the heartfelt strains which appear in the
vocal part; and still the instrumental part contains
nothing but a transformation of the leading motives.

Die Blu . . . . me

von Je . . . . ru . . . . . sa - lem.

More highly dramatic accents follow this lyric phrase,
leading to the reappearance of the second portion of the
first subject; but the principal melody is carried on
with increased animation, twice dwelling on the high
F *fortissimo* at the verse—

> " And mine is the guilt, mine the hell,
> This bosom's desolation dooming."

It concludes, however, *piano e morendo*, introducing
a noble cadence on F minor. The leading motives

from the prelude and first part now terminate this sublime tone-picture, forming an instrumental coda of six bars.

"Harald" (*Uhland*).

The bold knight Harald rides with his army through a wild forest: they sing many a victorious song, and carry on their shoulders many a captured flag. Loewe chose for the musical interpretation of this leading idea a very fine theme, which, both in its harmonisation and in its bright martial melody, distinctly indicates its source to have been of the Volkslied order, and is indeed substantially found in an Austrian popular song. Without referring its origin, however, to any particular Volkslied, we may say that it has in general the air of a song meant to be sung in chorus by a multitude of enthusiastic, patriotic soldiers. The frequent appearance of progressions in sixths, fifths, and thirds in the accompaniment, gives the theme a bright colour, as if produced by horns, and the Germanic character is well hit off in rhythm and mode (A flat, $\frac{4}{4}$):—

Alla marcia maestoso.
pomposo.

After a full cadence in A flat, to be played and sung
with *verve,* an *allegro leggiero* ($\frac{6}{8}$) in the key of the
dominant D flat appears, the fine, graceful, light dance-
melody of which fills eight bars of the prelude, and
wonderfully changes the last scene into one of fairy
spell and mysterious spirit-land :—

Allegro leggiero.

The accompaniment repeats this movement several
times, developing it in a charming fashion, following

the narrator, and yet taking its own course—painting
all details, as it were, with a fairy pencil.

This little phrase, representing the elves throwing
flowers round about, and their gradual subjection of the
warriors step by step, is lovely, and gives the pianist

ample scope for drawing out sweet tones from his instrument. The vocal part goes on in quieter, slower strides,
for the whole ballad is descriptive—good musical declamation and a fine *cantilene* being needful for its vocal
interpretation. As Loewe always makes his music
subserve entirely the poet's purposes, a change is
naturally given in tone and rhythm when the verses
refer to Harald's resistance. His harness protects him,
with bright steel, from head to foot, and his proud iron
will repels the elves' caresses. Firm, determined
chords hail his energy and self-control. The A flat
theme (we may call it the Harald-motive), transposed
into D flat and in $\frac{6}{8}$ time, accompanies his solitary ride
through the wood; all his warriors have become en-
chanted; the horses now run loose and wild. Suddenly
the whispering elf-melodies refill the air, but softer

than before, in higher octave, with somewhat altered figuration and a different accompaniment. Loewe wishes the pedal to be used for the eight introductory bars, in order to produce a confused but very interesting tone effect. A swarm of light-footed airy beings fills the trees, the water, the very air. Harald dismounts from his horse, takes off his armour, and drinks from the nearest spring. His destiny has overtaken him at last: he sits down on a rock; his strength fails; he falls asleep. These incidents are again painted with tones of an unfailing truth and a surprising descriptive power. One fragment only is here given, to show how fine the chord of the augmented

Durst ge - stillt, ver - sagt ihm Arm und Bein.

sixth suits the intended purpose. The dominant note leads to the reappearance of the Harald theme in A flat; but it is put in a lower octave, and has to be played *pianissimo*, as in a dream. Harald's magic

trance is, besides, marked by the vocal part being
based entirely on *one* note—*i.e.*, on the dominant E
flat, which gives to the final scene a mysterious pale

colour, overveiling the picture like a misty fog covering
a landscape. At the words—

> " When thunder growls and lightning flashes,
> Harald touches his sword hilt,"—

there is a *crescendo*, and the bass presents, instead of
chords, a *tremolo* accompaniment.

Loewe had, we here observe, as is evident in a thou-
sand other instances, a most refined instinct and feeling
for the adequate and appropriate means of expressing
the poet's hints and intentions. Towards the end, the
vocal part, after dwelling for eighteen bars on E flat,
emphasises the last words, "the old hero Harald," by
touching F flat,—a passing modulation, which expresses to perfection the tired, weary mood of the
king, who, like Barbarossa, still sits and sleeps on in

his old place as he has done for ages gone by, and will
do for ages to come :—

The vibrating bass motives die away in the stillness
of night and of repose. The three final bars contain
the harmony of A flat, but without the third of the
chord: this produces the horn effects of the Harald-
motive, as heard at a great distance.

" THE MOORISH PRINCE " (*Freiligrath*).

This grand poem of Freiligrath, containing a most
picturesque description of the fate of its hero, the
Moorish prince, was a fitting subject for Loewe's
genius. Although the poem is chiefly confined to narrative, it is from beginning to end full of dramatic life
and vigour. First, we see the prince armed for the
battle taking leave of his bride, and hurrying to the
stormy fight. Then we see the bride adorning herself

with pearls and flowers, waiting for her lover's return, whilst he is being made prisoner and sold to the hated Franks. Thereafter we see him at a circus in the midst of his foes, degraded, and compelled to play the part of a drummer. He never returns, alas! to his beloved Niger or his tent. This sad tale is told with great vividness and variety of mood and colour, introducing with each successive line a series of oriental pictures and glowing episodes, which no other composer than Loewe could have successfully ventured to represent in tone. Loewe divides the subject into three distinct ballads, taking the hint from the poet, who separates the main episodes, and leaving it to the imagination of the reader to fill up the space between the recorded facts —a task best performed by music, and affording ample scope for Loewe's distinctive talent. Loewe calls the first of these ballads " The Moorish Prince," the second, " The Moorish Princess," the third, " The Moorish Prince at the Circus." These three ballads may be sung in succession or singly, for they are separate tone-pictures with wonderful tragic cadences. Their mutual dependence is, however, maintained by their respective key-relation, as we find in the consecutive movements of works of greater dimensions.

The ballad No. I. (A minor, $\frac{3}{4}$, *vivace, non troppo*

allegro) introduces the prince's bold character by means
of an interesting prelude, the theme of which is treated
in the canon form, and carried by octave passages :—

The accompaniment, though written for pianoforte,
is yet really conceived in an orchestral form, and it is
later on frequently written in six or eight parts. The
chords accompanying the third and fourth line of the
first two verses are struck with rhythmic force, while
the clank of the swords is wonderfully indicated in the
interludes containing figures of sextuplets :—

The middle part of this ballad, in contrast with the former division, presents a more lyric strain in A major, accompanied in a somewhat softer, simpler manner. A cadence which reminds us of the overflowing melodic charm of southern love-songs terminates this subject, which deals with the prince's parting words to his bride :—

> " Adorn thee—see, pearls I bring thee :
> Prepare the feast, enwreath the cup."

The opening phrases of the first part in A minor reappear, but are treated in a different way: the octaves are in *arpeggio*, and give the motives a stormy, restless character. The climax of the ballad is, however, reached at the grand finale, where we find the most powerful musical accents, which are even singular and grotesque, given to the description of the battle-field soaked with blood; of the flight of lions and serpents, the rattling of drums bedecked with skulls, and the flag proclaiming death. The narrator recites these incidents, as it were, amidst a storm of excitement: the accompaniment expresses all details, the music speaks in fiery tongues.

L

The ballad thereafter bursts its bounds; even harmonic laws are, as it were, for a moment thrown aside —at least the following bars have alarmed many a theorist, and yet, after careful examination, they can be fully explained. The series of shakes, alternatively based on the four-stroked "" D sharp and E natural, are in direct harmonic contradiction with the melody sung between them and the accompanying chords below.

The resolution of the discords is, however, effected by the harmony of A minor, but it appears on the very last beat of each bar, as if hurriedly retrieving the neglect. The shakes obstinately take their own course, at one time appearing like changing notes, at another like substantive parts of the harmony. The effect is bewildering, but, owing to the extremely high, nearly toneless position of the shakes representing the clashing of the weapons, the dissonant intervals do not appear so striking as they would do if played in close harmony, or separated from the preceding and succeeding final phrases, which present pure and tranquil harmonic progressions. The whole part is a fine example of thematic work, forming a brilliant and sparkling finale. The postlude is made up of rapid passages, formed of thematic material to be executed with

verve and spirit. These passages rush down from the
highest octave to the lowest position in octaves, which
are ornamented at each beat by little shake-figures, as
if hurried on by whips, and tumbling over stones and
obstacles.

"The Moorish Princess."

The second ballad is written in A major (*adagio*, $\frac{12}{8}$),
and describes, with touching sweetness, the bride's pre-
parations for the return of her victorious lover. Can
there be anything more elegiac and poetic than the
trustful hope and devotion expressed in this and in
other parts of the melodious strain, appearing here in
the accompaniment?—

But they are soon hushed: we hear from afar the
noise of the battle; her heart throbs fast. The fierce
tones of the war-trumpet, beautifully rendered in the
instrumental score,—

are heard repeatedly, and give signals of alarm. The
sun stands high, the flowers wither, but she heeds it
not. Here the harmony changes, with fine modulations,
into the minor mode, and with fateful force the doleful
night comes on. A whispering and rustling among the
leaves interrupt the stillness of the sultry oriental
night; but she heeds it not. The crocodile creeps forward, seeking coolness beneath the palms, the lions roar
for their prey, and herds of elephants break through the
foliage. It is impossible to give by mere words an
idea of the extraordinary power of expression which
Loewe has displayed in his description of that terrible
night: one must play and sing the ballad bar by bar.
Beginning *pianissimo*, with a reminiscence of a theme
found in the first ballad, where the prince is said to step

forth from his tent, the instrumental part paints to perfection the twilight mood of the evening, when the glow-
worm's sparks fill the air. The bass growls like distant
thunder, introducing a *tremolo* figure, formed by major
and minor thirds, first ascending, then descending, but
mostly in chromatic progressions. The upper parts
present a peculiar little motive, which gives a coloured
lustre to the scene :—

The bass notes descend lower and lower ; their
motives expand by degrees from thirds into octaves,
ninths, and tenths,—

a trying part for the executant, demanding hands
like Liszt's. By-and-by animals and flowers sink
into sleep. An *allegro* ($\frac{4}{4}$) sets in, its minor mode
having been prepared for by the last descriptive
division :—

The well-accented quaver motive describes vividly
the hurry of the messenger who now approaches and
tells the maid of her princely Moor's defeat: " Lost the
battle, lost all hope; thy lover captured, taken to the
west, sold to the Franks over the sea !" In the music
which accompanies and follows this, we read all the pain
of the poor bride's tortured heart—

Her despair rings through the vast desert in wild
accents: she hides her cheeks in the glowing sand, and
tears the pearls from her head. With deep and woful
sighs, expressed in the accompaniment, this ballad
finishes in F sharp minor.

"The Moorish Prince at the Circus."

This ballad opens in the key of the first (A minor), $\frac{2}{4}$, but with an entirely new theme. It is a worthy third movement, bearing the brisk character of both a *scherzo* and a finale in the most concise form. We are in the circus, where every one has come to witness the horses' skill and the riders' bravery. The rhythm of this animated piece is that of a galop. The bass has a motive, which represents the curveting and the prancing of the horses, now heard loudly, now from a distance and confused. All parts which allude to the feast witnessed by the Moor are based upon the galop-theme,

which appears in various forms. In its first full development it modulates from A minor into brisk C
major, and so on. The noisy and animated music is
silenced by beautiful melancholy phrases which express the Prince's sad meditations. He stands behind
the door and gazes with tearless eye upon the Turkish drum, which he beats resignedly and mechanically.
The lion's skin—once adorning the Prince, now the prisoner, the slave—reminds him of his heroic deeds, his
noble sports. The accompaniment supports this section with energetic marked chords :—

Dass   er   im   Kam - pfe,   ge - schwun - gen   das   Schwert.

After each of the descriptive and declaimed verses
follows a little phrase of four bars for piano solo,
bringing in a section of the galop, by which we are
reminded of the doings in the circus, which the un-
happy Moor neither likes nor heeds :—

Touching beyond measure are the following poetic
phrases in E major, falling like sun‑rays into the
desolate circus mockery, drawing forth burning tears

Con molto affetto.

Und dass sie Blu‑men für ihn ge‑flückt.

dim.

Und dass sie . . . . das Haar ‑ ‑ mit Per ‑ ‑ ‑ len ge‑schmückt.

from the drummer's eyes. He thinks that *she* plucked
flowers for him, and for him adorned her hair with
pearls; but never did he return to his tent. We may
imagine how sweet and fascinating the beautiful melo‑
dious phrase, with the expressive dwelling on the G
sharp, must have sounded when sung with the com‑
poser's flexible tenor voice, and his inspired artistic
conception. Most interesting are the last eight bars,
both as to their harmonic effects and as to the unac‑
customed turn we find before the cadence. They rep‑

resent distinctly the Moor's despair and helpless rage. He beats the drum till, rattling, it bursts.

"EDWARD" (*translated by Herder*).

In the 'Lebensbilder' of Loewe's eldest daughter, Julie v. Bothwell, we find the following incidents narrated in connection with the creation of this weird grand ballad. C. M. Weber gave a concert in Halle when Loewe was still a student. Before the concert, Bergner, a schoolfellow of Loewe, recited to him the old Scottish ballad, "Edward," which Herder had translated into German. This ballad made a very deep impression upon Loewe. He, however, said nothing about it, but left his room and hastened to the concert, as he had promised Weber to turn the leaves for him. His beloved Julie Jacob was present in the concert-hall. Weber played his F minor concerto, and was so nervous that he missed a few bars, and the whole orchestra was put out for a moment: but young Loewe, who was seated near Weber, at once struck a few mighty chords on the piano, and continued playing, thus giving Weber an opportunity of putting his hands below Loewe's, and the concerto concluded amid tremendous applause. Loewe disappeared after the concerto; and his friends, missing him, went to his house, where they found him composing

the great ballad, " Edward." " I am happy to see you
again," said Bergner, "and must tell you that Miss
Jacob, after your disappearance, seemed not to take
interest in anything. I advise you to brighten with
a new composition the pale checks of your beloved."
" I have already composed a ballad," said Loewe ; " but
please let me alone, it is too late." The friends said
" Good night," and Bergner went to bed. Loewe
opened his window, and exclaimed, " How dark and
stormy the night !—dark and stormy like my music !"
He closed the windows and opened the piano, saying,
" Come out, little mouse, and hear how 'Edward' sounds."
He struck *fortissimo* the chord of E minor, and sang
with gradual *crescendo* that gloomy and dreadful ballad.
Suddenly a deep sigh was heard. Loewe looked round,
and saw at the door his friend Bergner in great excitement. Bergner exclaimed, " What are you doing ?
that is terrible ! I am trembling, and I am afraid of
you ; and ask you now, Are you a human being, and
what is your object ?" " At present," replied Loewe,
" I am the composer of 'Edward' ; to-morrow I shall
be the composer of the ' Erlking,' and that is already
something ; but you will soon see me in the pulpit !"
" I hope," said Bergner, " you will preach as well as you

sing." They went to bed; but the next day Bergner confessed that he had not been able to find peace in his soul until he had twice repeated the Lord's Prayer.

The very first chords beginning this ballad in E flat minor ($\frac{6}{8}$), and accompanying the anxious mother's question—

"Why does your brand sae drop wi' blude, Edward, Edward ?"[1]

and—

"Why sae sad gang ye, O ?"

are full of woe, and at once indicate the doom under which the two persons have fallen—the inevitable catastrophe impending over them.

This is effected by the wonderful harmonisation which Loewe's genius selected for the doleful strains

[1] This, like all other ballads of Loewe, is composed for the German words, but in quoting I use the English, and here the original Scotch version — Percy's Reliques of Ancient English Poetry, p. 82 (Sonnenschein).

which he lent to the mother's verses, and, moreover, to the lugubrious " O " which follows, as refrain, each strophe of that mighty national poem. Like a red thread visible amid the dark web of falsehood and guilt, there creeps a dissonant note through nearly all the chords which accompany the dialogue. In the very rhythm imparted to the mother's inquiries lies a certain restlessness with which the son's answers are contrasted by their reluctant, quiet mood, their time and melody :—

Ich hab' gesch la - gen mei - nen Geier todt,—

His explanations, we see, go hand in hand with falsehood. The vocal part intentionally makes octaves with the bass; and, to begin with, there is no third in the first chord, and every word has a hollow, strange sound and accent :—

> " I hae killed my hawk sae gude, mither, mither,
> And I hae nae mair but he, O !"

Then—

> "I hae killed my red-roan steed, mither,
>   That was sae fair and free, O !"

The mother's queries become more and more pressing, importing several very interesting variations in the musical treatment, until the son bursts forth with the full, overwhelming truth—

> "I hae killed my father dear, mither ;
>   Alas ! and wae is me, O !"

Loewe here introduces G minor, which, after the preceding parts in E flat minor with the repeated G flat, sounds as unprepared as it is wild, startling, and new. The time changes, too, from $\frac{6}{8}$ into $\frac{4}{4}$, giving the phrase a more accentuated breadth.

todt,   Mut . . . . ter   Mut - - - - ter, Ich

hab' ge - schla-gen mei-nen Va - - - - - - - - - ter todt.

The pianoforte evidently takes the place of a full orchestra, and supports the dramatic scene with adequate force, giving the vocal phrases, by a rich *tremolo*, a substantial foundation. The mother's inquiries after this confession, which, though foreseen, alarms and frightens her, are now set in a different form—

M

Und was wirst Du nun an dir thun, Edward, Ed-ward?

She tears open, so to speak, both her own wounds and
those of her son: she suspects the worst—she will
know all.   Again, and always in a new guise, the
dissonant intervals appear in a torturing, intruding
way.   The guilty mother now confronts the guilty son,
asking—

> " And quhatten penance will ye drie for that, Edward ? "

And his answers are full of despair and remorse, so
that we feel our soul rent in twain, and regard with
awe the creator of this dark and terrible tone-picture,
just as Loewe's friend Bergner did.   How beautiful
and majestic is Loewe's conception of the son's resolution—

> " I'll set my feet in yonder boat, mither,
>   And I'll fare over the sea, O ! "

will wan-dern üb . . . . . er's Meer!

O!

The melody expands into vast forms, the instrument mourns with him upon whose guilty but repentant soul a world of woe weighs heavy. A single ray of light falls into this night of grief, when the mother speaks of his "towers and ha' that were sae fair to see"; but it is suppressed by the son's gloomy reply—

"I'll let them stand till they doon fa',
For here nevir mair maun I be, O!"

New and still more energetic accents are found for these words. He is condemning himself to frantic self-destruction—

Ach nim - mer   steh's   und   sink,   und   fall!

The descending passage, characterising the "down-
fa'" of his estates, is particularly fine and interesting.
The mother's breast heaves deep and quick.

"And what will ye leave to your bairns and wife, Edward?"

she stammers and moans; and the son is cruel in his
answer—

"The world's room—let thame beg through life!"

Entirely new musical means are again employed for
this verse. The music turns to the key of E flat
major—which, however, is very soon left, and minor
harmonies reappear. Then, after the mother's trembling
last words—

"And quhat will ye leave to your ain mither dear?"—

Und   was   soll dei . . . . . ne

Mut - ter thun.   Ed - ward,   etc.

etc.

the final blow is dealt. A thunderbolt falls on her ears
and ours—

"The curse of hell frae me sall ye bear!"

cries he with mad wrath and anguish.

Der Fluch der Höl - - - - - - - - - - - - le soll

auf euch ruh'n; Mut - - - - - - ter,

Loewe lends this scene his strongest accents and colours, striking the key of E flat minor, and giving the vocal phrases a heavier instrumental support than at

the corresponding former $\frac{4}{4}$ division. The chords figured in semiquavers, and in contrary motion, have to
be played with vigour and *fortissimo*, the climax being
reached at the reappearance of the same phrase, a semi-
tone higher (F flat), at which the accompaniment occupies
the extreme limits of the pianoforte compass. It takes
our breath away to hear how this son curses his mother.
It is not only the elementary dynamic force which
makes us tremble and fear with the guilty, but it is
the power of the idea transformed by Loewe into music
of truly classical grandeur—into an overpowering episode
unfolded before our eyes. The last words of the son,
" Sic counsels ye gave to me," are to be declaimed with
dramatic accentuation, reminding us, in its vigour and
power, of the best declamatory phrases from Wagner's
dramas. A last despairing " Oh " concludes the curse.

" ODIN'S RIDE OVER THE SEA " (*Schreiber*).

The relationship between Wagner's and Loewe's spirit
in their formation of motives is perhaps more perceiv-
able in this ballad than in any other of Loewe's works.
The subject is northern, and Wagner's true element
was, as is well known, the northern mythology. This

accounts for the likeness of musical ideas, which
sprang from the same poetic source. We find in this
ballad of Loewe, Odin, Oluf the smith, the eagles, the
war-horse,—corresponding to Wotan, Mime the smith,
the ravens, and the Walkyrie horse, in Wagner's
famous "Nibelungen." It is clear that Loewe could
not have been inspired by Wagner's drama, as Loewe
composed his ballad "Odin" on a journey to Norway
in the year 1851, when Wagner's "Nibelungen"
had not yet been published. The original sharp
clear northern colour is splendidly hit off in this
ballad, written in E minor. We discover in it only
manly energetic motives, and harmony of solid metal.
The first narrative part deals with the smith's movements, and the knocking at his door heard at midnight; the wind howls on the sea-shore, and Master
Oluf hastens to open the door. Odin's appearance and
speeches are expressed in heroic, majestic phrases. A
giant stands before us, and we sympathise with the smith's
awe and wonder. Several incidents are illustrated in a
very realistic fashion, so that even the layman in music
might guess the meaning by the effect produced—for
instance, the knocking at the smith's door represented
by this plastic motive—

mit Macht, he - - raus!

and the rapid figure of demi-semiquavers employed in the representation of the swiftness of Odin's horse.

Mein Rap - - - pe, der läuft wohl mit dem Wind.

We may remark Loewe's wonderfully expressive way of illustrating the words, "The horse-shoe stretched itself," by actually extending the last chords of this phrase in the imitation: first the chords of C natural are put in close and then in extended harmony. The result is, that this incident gains all the significance of an event passing before our own eyes — it is a splendid specimen of *plastic* tone-painting.

Thereafter begins softly, but more and more *crescendo*,
an uproar, raging like a storm in all parts: we think
involuntarily of the awe felt by the dwarf Mime
(in Wagner's "Siegfried") on seeing the red light
which Wotan had left behind him, indicating the
recent presence of the god. Loewe introduces after
this a beautiful warrior-like theme in E minor, realis-
ing the verse, "The rider mounts with clanging sword."
After each second bar, containing a vocal phrase, the
accompaniment repeats it after the fashion of the refrain found in old student songs. The time changes
after this from $\frac{4}{4}$ to $\frac{6}{8}$, each beat of the bar containing a triplet figure, which is executed partly in unison,
partly in contrary motion, rushing up and down the
keyboard, exhausting in its course the attendant keys
of A minor, and representing wonderfully the flight of
Odin's horse, and the twelve eagles following but never
overtaking him.

Dwelling in the highest octave on the harmony of F
and C, the triplet motive is carried on, giving a brilliant
puzzling effect to the words, "A red glory surrounds
Odin's head."

This is a veritable "fire-spell" in miniature, conceived
in an orchestral form. The rapid passages are now
carried out by one part of the accompaniment only,
whilst the bass has this mighty motive, which first
appears in the vocal part, sounding like a trumpet-blast.

Very noble and majestic is the last vocal phrase. It
is preceded by an illustrative figure, which appears in
the accompaniment, and is based on the harmony of
the diminished seventh (a chord which, by the by,
plays as prominent a part in Loewe's works as it does
in Wagner's scores), and which leads to a full cadence
in E minor.

The triplet figures, based on arpeggio chords of E minor and its dominant, intermixed with chromatic notes, now reappear, and execute a fine instrumental *finale* of five bars.

"Odin's Ride over the Sea" is one of my favourite ballads; and I was happy to see, on the occasion of my singing it before an Edinburgh audience, that it impressed them very much. It was with feelings of peculiar pleasure, accordingly, that I found myself, shortly after my Loewe concert in Edinburgh, the recipient of the actual original manuscript of this ballad, which was presented to me by Frau Julie von Bothwell *née* Loewe.

"The Three Songs" (*Uhland*).

King Sifried sits in his large and crowded hall. "Which of you harpers," he asks, "knows the finest song?" A youth steps forward, with harp in hand, and his sword at his side. "Three songs I know," he says; "the first thou surely hast long forgotten—'Thou hast killed my brother; and oh! my brother!' The second song I have made in a dark and stormy night—

'Thou shalt fight with me for life and death—for life and death.'" The minstrel lays aside his harp, and the king and he fight with frenzy wild and long, until King Sifried falls in his spacious hall. "Now," cries the harper, "I sing the third and most beautiful song, —'King Sifried lies in his red blood—lies in his red, red blood!'"

These highly dramatic incidents are worked out in Loewe's masterly style with truthfulness and brilliant effect. The ballad, written in F sharp minor (*allegro assai* $\frac{4}{4}$), is one of Loewe's earliest works (Op. 3), and is marked by that dramatic vigour which is characteristic of this period. It offers no ordinary difficulty both to the vocalist and to the pianist. It demands great technical abilities and enthusiasm, particularly in carrying out the instrumental parts, which are rich in tone and colour, and depict with plastic motives and figures the leading idea of revengeful fighting, which passes before us with the fury of a hurricane. The first verse is carried out in the style of an introduction. It characterises with festal tones the exalted mood of the king and his noble guests.

The following passage contains declamatory phrases which proceed in octaves, and in an animated, abrupt rhythm. The dramatic scenes are introduced with the words, "Three songs I know" ("Drei Lieder weiss ich").

Loewe modulates here characteristically into D major. Most interesting and illustrative is the following phrase, which occurs first in D minor and then in G minor. Accentuated octaves appearing in the accompaniment seem actually to deal blows as with sharp-pointed weapons.

Mei - nen Bru · · · · · · · · · · · der

hast du meuch lings er · · · sto - chen

und a . . . . . ber, hast du . . . . . .

The dramatic and descriptive parts of the song modulate frequently, and offer a fine example of Loewe's skill in working out his themes, often combining two or three leading motives, and always achieving the desired effect. Very menacing and determined is the minstrel's challenge—

"Musst mit mir fech . . . . . ten, auf

Le · · · ben und Ster · · · · ben!"

A fine *crescendo* thereafter illustrates the actual fight
between the king and the harper.   The accompaniment
in these parts realises, so to speak, all that is told by
the narrator in the vocal part, and represents with
unmistakable expression the crossing of arms, and the
two deadly blows which strike Sifried to the ground.
(See bars 9 and 11 of the following example.)

Da

legt' er die Har - - fe wohl auf den Tisch, und sie

zo - - - - gen bei - - - - - de die Schwer - - ter

frisch, und foch - - - - - - - - - - - - - - - - - - ten

A new subject, prepared by the harmony of C sharp minor and major, appears when the third song is referred to, and in this the key of F sharp major is introduced—a key very well suited for expressing the joyful victory of the harper.

Nun sing ich das drit-te und

schön · · · · ste   Lied,   8va · · · · · · · · · · ·

Ped.

Das   werd'   ich   nim · mer.

etc.

The final words, " Sifried lies in his red, red blood,"
are set in a lower position, and are accompanied by
lugubrious tones, whilst the peculiar refrain, " and oh!"
(" und aber!") which occurs after some of the former
verses, receives a still more emphasised rendering here.
The final phrases modulate back into the attendant key
of F sharp minor, and a brilliant coda in the piano
parts with the bright harmony of F sharp major terminates this wonderful ballad.

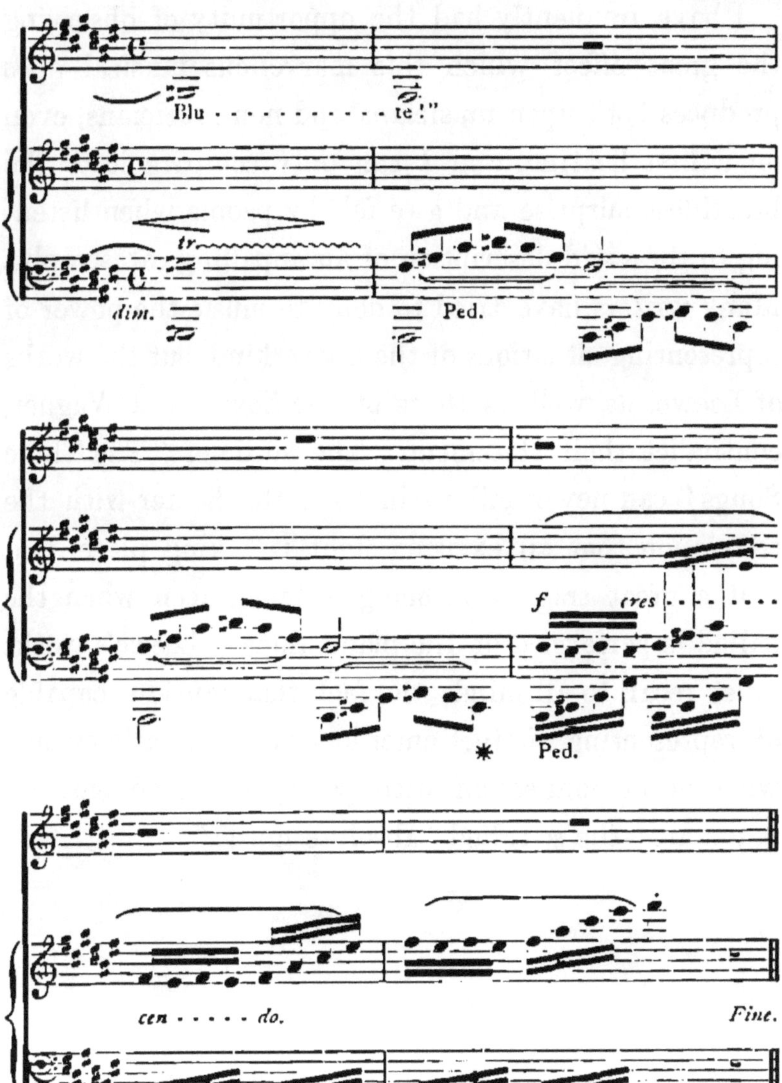
Blu
te!"
tr
dim.
Ped.
f
cres
Ped.
cen
do.
Fine.

I have frequently had the opportunity of observing the great effect which this marvellous musical epos produces both upon musicians and non-musicians, even on a first hearing, and I can only compare it to the breathless surprise and awe felt by people when listening to the vivid description of an appalling catastrophe. Many writers have tried to deny to music the power of representing situations of the above kind, but the works of Loewe, as well as those of Beethoven and Wagner, contradict their statement. The music of " The Three Songs " can never fail to impress the hearer with the conviction that an exciting fight is taking place, and that a great tragedy is being enacted, even when the ballad is performed on the piano alone. Loewe's works must recall to all minds the fact that music *is* capable of representing distinct emotions and dramatic events, whether in connection with poetry or as an emancipated art—the so-called " absolute music."

APPENDIX.

BERLIN PAULSTRASSE 9,
8 *January* 1890.

MY DEAR SIR,—Accept my warmest thanks for your amiable letter, and the kind New-Year's wishes, which I return with all my heart.

I hasten to reply to the most important question in your letter. Richard Wagner's opinion of Loewe has as yet only been communicated to the public through me. My authority is not literary but oral. I know it from the mouth of trustworthy men who were on terms of intimate friendship with Wagner. That Wagner very highly appreciated Loewe's ballads, "The Mother's Ghost," "Elvershöh," I have learned from the late Frau Dr. Heinrich von Stein. Wagner's judgment concerning "Edward" I learned from Eugen Gura. The same was reported to me a year ago by Wagner's niece, Frau Johanna Jachman-Wagner, and also the fact that Wagner himself very often sang with enthusiasm "Edward" and "Das Hochzeitlied," which also he thought very highly of. In the year 1881 Wagner went through a whole series of Loewe's ballads with a professor of music from Munich, and showed an enthusiastic love for them : amongst these ballads was "The Great Christoph." Professor Julius Hey, now in Berlin, has told me, and authorised me to refer to his testimony, that Wagner often spoke with great admiration of Loewe's ballads. Wagner is reported by Professor Hey to have once said in so many words to his pupils : " Now, my young friends (*kinderchen*), you think Schubert's ' Erlking ' to be the best ? Listen ! here is one much finer,—it is that by Loewe. Schubert's ' Erlking ' is not quite true, but Loewe's is true !" Wagner, in conversation with musicians, has frequently drawn their attention to Loewe, and thus the master has worked for him. Gura's love for Loewe is, for instance, entirely due to Wagner's influence. . . .

With hearty greetings, yours faithfully,

DR. M. RUNZE.

ALBERT B. BACH, Esq.

LETTER OF FRL. EVA WAGNER TO ALBERT B. BACH, EDINBURGH.

MY DEAR SIR,—My mother is so very busy just now that I have to answer your letter.

My father has indeed directed the attention of Gura to Loewe's Ballads, and he sang some to us in the Villa Wahn-fried.

My father's sympathy was, however, chiefly directed to Loewe's earlier compositions, published in one volume, containing "Edward," "Erlkönig," "Wirthin Töchterlein," and some others.

The anecdote concerning my grandfather Liszt [see page 79, "The Mother's Ghost"] appears to me correct. . . .
Yours,   EVA WAGNER.

BAYREUTH, WAHNFRIED, May 1, '90.

BIBLIOGRAPHY.

(h. *high* ; l. *low* ; m. *medium voice.*)

SCHLESINGERS MUSIKHANDLUNG (Rob. Lienau), BERLIN.

Op.

1. Drei Balladen (Three Ballads). Composed 1818 ; published 1824 :—
   1. Edward (Herder). Schottische Ballade. (m. l.)
   2. Der Wirthin Töchterlein (Uhland). (h. m. l.)
   3. Erlkönig (Goethe). (h. m. l.)
2. Drei Balladen, published 1824 :—
   1. Treuröschen (Körner). (h. m.)
   2. Herr Oluf (Herder). (h. m. l.)
   3. Walpurgisnacht (Alexis). (m.)
3. Drei Balladen. Published 1825 :—
   1. Abschied (Uhland). (h. m.)
   2. Elvershöh (Herder). (h.)
   3. Die drei Lieder (Uhland). (m.)
4. Hebräische Gesänge, Gesichte und Balladen. (Hebrew Melodies, Lord Byron.) Published 1826.
   Heft I. :—
   1. Herodes' Klage um Mariamne.
   2. An den Wassern zu Babel. (m.)
   3. Wär' ich wirklich so falsch. (m.)
   4. Alles ist eitel. (m.)
   5. Todtenklage. (m.)
   6. Thränen und Lächeln. (h.)
5. Heft II. :—
   1. Sie geht in Schönheit. (h.)

    2. Jephta's Tochter. (h.)
    3. Die wilde Gazelle. (h.)
    4. Weint um Israel. (m.)
    5. Mein Geist ist trüb'. (m.)
 7. Zwei Balladen. Published 1827 :—
    1. Die Spreenorne. (h.)
    2. Der späte Gast (Alexis.)
 8. Zwei Balladen. Published 1827 :—
    1. Goldschmieds Töchterlein (Uhland). (h. m. l.)
    2. Der Mutter Geist (Talvj). Composed 1824. Alt Schot-
       tische Ballade. (m.)
13. Hebräische Gesänge. Heft III.
14. Hebräische Gesänge. Heft IV. Published 1826. (h. m.)
20. Drei Balladen (Goethe) :—
    1. Hochzeitlied. (h. m.)
    2. Der Zauberlehrling. (m.)
    3. Die wandelnde Glocke. (h. m.)
21. Die Gruft der Liebenden Ballade.
33. Legenden (Legends) :—
    1. Jungfrau Lorenz. (h.)
    2. Das heilige Haus. (h.)
    3. Des fremden Kindes. (h. m.)
34. Legende : Der Grosse Christoph.
49. Drei Balladen aus dem Polnischen. (Three Ballads from the
    Polish of Mizkiewitsch.)
50. Zwei Balladen aus dem Polnischen. (Two Ballads from Mizkie-
    witsch.)
63. Zwei Gesänge. (Two songs of Marggraff.)
64. Vier Fabellieder. (h. m.)
78. Drei Balladen :—
    1. Jungfräulein Annica.
    2. Die verlorne Tochter.
    3. Bulmenballade.
85. Mahomeds Gesang (Goethe). (h.)
86. Mein Herz ich will dichfragen (Halm). (h.)
88. Gesang der Geister über den Wassern Ode (Goethe), für Ten.,
    Sop., Alt, und Bass.
89. Sechs Lieder (Delia Helena). (h.)
93. Meerfahrt Ballade (Freiligrath). (m.)
95. Alpins Klage um Morar (Goethe). (m.)

112. Schottische Bilder für Clarinette und Pianoforte.
112*a*. Des Glockenthürmers Töchterlein (Rückert). (h. m.)
113. Noch ahnt man Raum der Sonne Licht (Uhland). Duet, Sop. und Tenor.
114. Der Mönch zu Pisa Ballade (Vogl). (m. l.)
115. Der gefangene Admiral Ballade. (l. m.)
118. Odin's Meeresritt oder der Schmied auf Helgoland Ballade (Schreiber). (m.) Composed 1851 ; published 1854.
119. Lied der Königin Elisabeth (translated by Herder). (h.)
120. Die Hochzeit der Thetis Cantate für Solo und Chor (Schiller). Published 1851.
123. Drei Gesänge :—
    1. Sängers Gebet. (h.)
    2. Trommelständchen. (h.)
    3. Die Uhr (also with English words). (h. m. l.)
125. Drei Balladen für eine Bass-stimme :—
    1. Landgraf Philipp.
    2. Das Vaterland.
    3. Der alte Schiffsherr.
126. Sanct Helena Ballade (Kahlert). (m.) Published 1859.
127. Der kleine Schiffer. (h.)
128. Archibald Douglas (Fontane). (h. m. l.) (With English words.) Published 1858.
129. Drei Balladen :—
    1. Der Teufel.
    2. Der Nöck.
    3. Die Schwanen Jungfrau.
130. Liedergabe. Heft I. (h.) Heft II. (h.)
131. Die Heilung des Blindgebornen. (Oratorio with Organ or Pianoforte.)
137. Vier Phantassien f. Pianoforte :—
    1. Der Abschied.
    2. Meerfahrt.
    3. Die neue Heimath.
    4. Die Prairie.
141. Der seltene Beter Ballade. (h. m. l.)
142. Der Traum der Wittwe Legende (Rückert). (m.)
144. Spirito Santo. (h. l. m.)
145. Fünf Lieder. (m. h. l.)
 25. Die Walpurgisnacht (Goethe). Für Solo und Chor mit Orchester, und für Chorstimmen.

125. Drei Balladen for a Bass voice :—
 1. Landgraf Philipp (Kopisch). (m. l.)
 2. Das Vaterland (Vogl). (l.)
 3. Der alte Schiffsherr (Vogl). (l. m.)
Dr Carl Loewes Selbstbiographie für die Öffentlichkeit bearbeitet
von C. H. Bitter. Berlin, 1870 (Schlesinger).

Schlesinger has published with English words " Die Uhr " (" The
Clock ") (m.) and " Archibald Douglas " (m.) ; and will shortly
publish several ballads by Loewe with English words.

HOFMEISTER, Leipzig.

Op.
6. Wallhaide Ballade (Körner). (h.)
9. Gesammelte Gesänge, Romanzen und Balladen. Published 1828:—
 Heft I. Nachtgesänge. (m.)
  1. Die Lotosblume (Heine). (m.)
  2. Der König auf dem Thurme. (m.)
  3a. Nachtlied (Goethe). Über allen Gipfeln. (m.)
  3b. Nachtlied (Goethe). Der du von dem Himmel bist. (h.)
  4. Geisterleben (Uhland). (m.)
  5. Die Elfenkönigin (Matthison). (h.)
 Heft II. Nachtgesänge :—
  1. Todtengräberlied aus Hamlet (Shakespeare). (l.)
  2. Lied der Desdemona aus Othello (Shakespeare). (m.)
  3. Die Abgeschiedenen (Uhland). (h.)
  4. Das Ständchen (Uhland). (m.)
  5. Die Jungfrau und der Tod (Kugler). Duo für Sop.
   und Bass.
 Heft III. Gesänge der Sehnsucht :—
  1. Ich denke dein (Goethe). (h.)
  2. Meine Ruh' ist hin (Goethe, ' Faust '). (h.)
  3. Wie der Tag mir schleicht (Rousseau). (h.)
  4. Der Treuergebene. (h.)
  5. Die Sehnsucht (Goethe).
 Heft IV. Gesänge der Sehnsucht :—
  1. Wenn du warst mein eigen (Kosegarten). (h.)
  2. Abschied (Gerstenberg). (h.)
  3. Frühlingserwachen (Gramberg). (h.)

4. Ihr Spaziergang (Talvj). (h.)
5. Graf Eberhards Weissdorn (Uhland). (m.)
Heft V. Heitere Gesänge:—
  1. Minnelied (Voss).
  2. Hans und Grethe (Uhland).
  3. Bauernregel (Uhland). (m.)
  4. Die Zufriedenen (Uhland). (h.)
  5. An die fleissige Spinnerin. (h.)
Heft VI. Heitere Gesänge:—
  1. Wach auf. (h.)
  2. Liebesgedanken (Müller). (h.)
  3. Vogelsang (Tieck). h.
  4. Mädchen sind wie der Wind. (m.)
  5. Graf Eberstein (Uhland). (m.)
Heft VII. Sechs Gedichte:—
  1. Der Pilgrim v. St Just (Platen).
  2. Im Traume sah ich die Geliebte (Heine). (m.)
  3. Erste Liebe (Heine). (m.)
  4. Neuer Frühling (Heine). (h.)
  5. Du schönes Fischermädchen (Heine). (m.)
  6. Ich hab im Traum geweinet (Heine). (m.)
Heft VIII. Fünf Gedichte aus Goethe's Nachlass:—
  1. Thurmwächter. (m.)
  2. Lynceus. (m.)
  3. Lynceus der Thürmer.
  4. Mädchenwünsche.
  5. Gutmann und Gutweib.
Heft IX. Sechs Lieder:—
  1. Scene aus Goethe's Faust, " Ach neige." (h.)
  2. Der alte Goethe. (m.)
  3. Die verliebte Schäferin (Goethe).
  4. An Aphrodite (Ode der Sappho).
  5. An di Grille (Ode des Anakreon).
  6. Der Fernen (Gerstenberg).
Heft X. Sechs Lieder:—
  1. Jugend ünd Alter. (Hoffmann v. Fallersleben). (m.
  2. Sylphide (Herder). (h.)
  3. Der Bräutigam. (h.)
  4. Niemand hats gesehen. (m.)
  5. Einrichtung. (h.)
  6. Der Apotheker als Nebenbuhler (Gruppe). (m.)

30. Die Zerstörung von Jerusalem (The Destruction of Jerusalem).
Great oratorio. Composed 1829; published 1832.
35. Legenden. Heft III. : 1. Johanniswürmchen. (m.) 2. Johann
v. Nepomuk. (h.)
36. Legenden. Heft IV.
39. Der Bergmann Liederkreis (Giesebrecht).
45. Zwei Balladen :—
    1. Harald (Uhland). Published 1835.
    2. Madahöh (Goethe). (m.)
52. Esther Liederkreis in Balladenform (Giesebrecht).   (h.m.)
53. Alpenphantasie für Pianoforte, A moll.
54. Der Sturm von Alhama spanische Romanze.   (h.)
68. Drei Balladen (Freiligrath) :—
    1. Schwalbenmärchen.   (h.)
    2. Der Edelfalk.   (h.)
    3. Der Blumen Rache.   (h.)   Published 1839.
69. Gerstenbergs nachgelassene Gedichte.   (h. m.)
99. Kaiser Karl V.   Vier historische Balladen :—
    1. Das Wiegenfest zu Gent.   (m.)
    2. Kaiser Karl V.   (m.)
    3. Der Pilgrim v. St Just.   (l.)
    4. Die Leiche v. St Just (Grün.)

PETERS, LEIPZIG.

Op.
107a. Zigeunersonate für Pianoforte :—
    1. Indisches Mährchen.
    2. Zigeunertauz.
    3. Abendcultus.
56. Drei Balladen (Vogl) :—
    1. Heinrich der Vogler.
    2. Der Gesang.
    3. Urgrossvater's Gesellschaft
65. Drei Balladen (Vogl) : —
    1. Das vergessene Lied.   (h.
    2. Das Erkennen.   (h).
    3. Wittekind.   (m.)
67. Drei historische Balladen :—
    1. Der Feldherr.   (h.)

    2. Die Glocken zu Speier. (m.)

    3. Landgraf Ludwig. (m.)

70. Feuersgedanken. (m.)

79. Vierstimmige Gesänge für Sop., Alt, Ten., und Bass (Goethe und Keferstein).

80. Mehrstimmige Gesänge :—

    Drei Gesänge für Sop., Alt, Ten., und Bass.

    Zwei Gesänge für drei Frauenstimmen.

91. Heilig, Heimlich ! (Grubitz). Duett für Sop. und Ten.

94. Zwei Balladen :—

    1. Die Ueberfahrt (Uhland). (m.)

    2. Die schwarzen Augen (Vogl). (m.)

98. Der Graf v. Habsburg Ballade (Schiller).

100. Psalm 23.

101. Psalm 121.

102. Psalm 33.

116. Drei Balladen :—

    1. Die Dorfkirche (Zedlitz). (h.)

    2. Der Alte König (Vogl).

    3. Der Mummelsee.

17. Der Gang nach dem Eiserhammer Ballade (Schiller). (h.) (Out of print.)

C. A. CHALLIER & Co., Berlin.

Op.

11. Abend-Fantasie für Pianoforte.

15. Sechs Serbenlieder (translated by Talvj). (Six Servian Songs).

16. Grosse Sonate Edur für Pianoforte.

19. Sechs Gesänge für fünf und vier Männerstimmen. (Six Songs for four and five male voices.)

22. Zehn geistliche Gesänge (Ten Sacred Songs).

23. Die nächtliche Heerschau Ballade (Zedlitz). (With French words by Mery and Barthélemy.) (m.) Composed 1832 ; published 1833.

24. Drei Quartette für zwei Violinen, Viola, und Violoncello in G dur, F dur, and B dur. (Out of print.)

27. Mazeppa Tondichtung nach Byron für Pianoforte.

28. Der barmherzige Bruder für Pianoforte.

29. Die Braut von Corinth Ballade (Goethe). (h.)
31. Stimmen der Elfen. 3 Duettinen für Sopr. und Alt.
32. Grand Sonate elegique F moll Pianoforte
40. Die eherne Schlange (The Brazen Serpent). Oratorio for male
voices (Giesebrecht).
43. Drei Balladen :—
    1. Der Fischer (Goethe). (h.) Composed 1835; pub-
lished 1835.
    2. Der Räuber (Uhland). (m.)
    3. Das nussbraune Mädchen (Herder). (h.)
48. Die Apostel von Philippi (The Apostles of Philippi). Oratorio
for male voices (Giesebrecht).
57. Fünf Oden des Horaz für 4 Männerstimmen (Übersetzt Voss).
60. Frauenliebe Liederkranz (Chamisso). (m.)
61. Zwei Balladen (Alexis). For one or four voices.
    1. Fredericus Rex.
    2. General Schwerin.

BREITKOPF & HÄRTEL, Leipzig.

Op.
10. Bilder des Orients. (H. Stieglitz). Published 1834.
    Erster Kranz. Wanderbilder. (h. m.)
    Zweiter Kranz. Bilder der Heimat. (h. m.)
44. Drei Balladen von Goethe :—
    1. Der Bettler.
    2. Der getreue Eckardt.
    3. Der Todtentanz.
58. Paria von Goethe :—
    Gebet : Grosser Brama. (h.)
    Legende. Wasser holen geht die reine. (h.)
    Dank : Grosser Brama. (m.)
59. Drei Balladen von Goethe :—
    1. Wirkung in der Ferne.
    2. Der Sänger.
    3. Der Schatzgräber.
75. Legenden für eine Altstimme (Legends for alto voice).
81. Fünf Lieder fur Sop., Alt, Tenor, und Bass. Partitur und
Stimmen.

A. CRANZ, BRESLAU.

Op.
97. Drei Balladen (Freiligrath), published 1844 :—
    1. Der Mohrenfürst. (h.)
    2. Die Mohrenfürstin. (h.)
    3. Der Mohrenfürst auf der Messe. (h.)
124. Der letzte Ritter. Drei Balladen (Grün) :—
    1. Max in Augsburg. (m.)
    2. Max und Dürer. (m.)
    3. Abschied. (m.)
136. Nebo, Ballade (Freiligrath). (m.)
134. Agnete, Ballade (Plönnies).

BOTE & BOCK, BERLIN.

Op.
62. Rückerts Gedichte.
77. Te Deum für Chor und Orchester.
82. Johann Huss. Oratorio (Zenne).
83. Die Heizelmänchen (Kopisch). (h.)
84. Fünf Humoresken für vier Männerstimmen.
92. Prinz Eugen der edle Ritter Ballade (Freiligrath). (m.)
96. Biblische Bilder für Pianaforte :—
    1. Bethesda.
    2. Gang nach Emaus.
    3. Martha und Maria.

BACHMANN, HANOVER.

Op.
104. Drei Lieder. (Goethe). Duette für zwei Sopr. or zwei Bässe :—
    1. Die Freude.
    2. An Sami.
    3. März.

109. Die verfallene Mühle Ballade (Vogl).
110. Am Klosterbrunnen (Vogl).
Wolkenbild (Locper).

HEINRICHSHOFEN, Magdeburg.

Op.
132. Die Auferweckung des Lazarus (The Awakening of Lazarus).
(With German and English words.)   Vocal Oratorio.
140. Die Gottesmauer (Rückert).   Ballade.   (h.)
122. Kaiser Heinrich's IV. Waffenwacht (Schwab).
108. Zwei Balladen (Vogl) :—
      1. Der Schützling.   (m.)
      2. Hueska.   (m.)

SCHOTT, Mainz.

Op.
27. Legenden :
      1. Muttergottesbild.   (m.)
      2. Moosröslein.   (m.)
      3. Das Paradies in der Wüste.
38. Gregor auf dem Stein Legende (Kugler).   (h.)
46. Die Siebenschläfer (The Seven Sleepers).   Oratorio (Giesebrecht).
55. Gutenberg.   Oratorio (Giesebrecht).
66. Die Festzeiten (Church Feast Days).   Sacred Oratorio.

LEUCKART, Breslau.

Op.
111. Der Papagei : humoristische Ballade (Rückert) für 4 Männerstimmen (for four male voices).
Stimmen (for S. A. T. B.)
Für eine Singstimme (the same arranged for solo voice).

LITOLFF.

Op.
106. Die Reigerbeize, Ballade (Grün). (m.)
120a. Die Begegnung am Meeresstrande (The Meeting on the Sea-
shore). With English words (Pick). (h.)

FÜRSTNER.

Op.
121. Zwei Balladen :—
1. Kaiser Otto's Weihnachtsfeier (Muller). (l.)
2. Der Drachenfels (Lütze). (h.)

BAHN.

Op.
18. Grosses Duo für das Pianoforte zu vier Händen.
26. Quatuor spirituel für zwei Violinen, Viola, und Violoncello.
71. Kleiner Haushalt (Rückert). (m.)

SIMROCK, BONN.

Op.
41. Sonate brillante für Pianoforte.
42. Die drei Wünsche komisches Singspiel von Raupach (out of
print). Daraus einzeln : Overture für Orchester.
Piano à 2 ms. and à 4 ms.

AD. BRAUER.

Op.
73. Zwei lyrische Fantasien :—
1. Die Göttin im Putzzimmer (Rückert).
2. Die Zugvögel (Tegnér).
135. Tom der Reimer (Thomas the Rhymer). (m.)

BAUER, BRAUNSCHWEIG.

Op.
103. Drei Lieder :—
  1. Gruss vom Meere (Fürst Schwanzenberg).
  2. Menschenlose (Franke).
  3. Deutsche Barcarole.
105. Tod und Tödin Ballade (Tschabuschigg).
133. Der Asra Ballade (Heine). (h.)

LOEWE-ALBUM. SELECTED BALLADS AND SONGS OF LOEWE.

IN SEVEN VOLUMES.

Band I. *Balladen.* Peters' Edition.—Heinrich der Vogler. Landgraf Ludwig. Die Glocken zu Speier. Das Erkennen. Der Graf von Habsburg. Die nächtliche Heerschau. Der Mohrenfürst. Friedericus Rex. Der Fischer. Der kleine Haushalt Mk. 3
Band II. *Balladen.* Peters' Edition. — Schwalbenmärchen. Der Edelfalk. Der Blumen Rache. Harald. Graf Eberstein. Das Wiegenfest zu Gent. Carl V. in Wittenberg. Der Pilgrim von St Just. Die Leiche zu St Just. In die Ferne . Mk. 3
Band III. *Balladen.* Schlesinger's Edition.—Edward. Der Wirthin Töchterlein. Erlkönig. Herr Oluf. Goldschmied's Töchterlein. Prinz Eugen. Des Glockenthürmers Töchterlein. Die Uhr. Archibald Douglas . . . . Mk. 4
Band IV. *Balladen.* Schlesinger's Edition.—Abschied. Elvershöh. Die drei Lieder. Hochzeitlied. Jungfrau Lorenz. Der grosse Christoph. Der Mönch zu Pisa . . Mk. 4
Band V. 23 *Hebräische Gesänge und Balladen nach Byron.* Schlesinger's Edition. (Mit einem Vorwort von Dr Max Runze.)— Herodes' Klage um Mariamne. An den Wassern zu Babel. Wär' ich wirklich so falsch ? Alles ist eitel, spricht der Prediger. Todtenklage. Thränen und Lächeln. Sie geht in Schönheit. Jephta's Tochter. Die wilde Gazelle. Weint um Israel.

Mein Geist ist trüb'. Saul vor seiner letzten Schlacht. Sanherib's Niederlage. Belsazar's Gesicht. Die höh're Welt. Jordan's Ufer. Wohin, o Seele? Die Sonne der Schlaflosen. Saul und Samuel. Elipha's Gesicht. David's Harfe. Saul. Jerusalem's Zerstörung . . . . Mk. 4
Band VI. *Balladen.* Schlesinger's Edition.—Treu Röschen. Die wandelnde Glocke. Des fremden Kindes heiliger Christ. Der heilige Franziscus. Meerfahrt. Der gefangene Admiral. Der selt'ne Beter. Der Junggesell. Odin's Meeres-Ritt Mk. 4
Band VII. *Balladen.* Schlesinger's Edition.—Der späte Gast. Die Gruft der Liebenden. Die verlorene Tochter. Trommel-Ständchen. Landgraf Philipp. Der alte Schiffsherr. Spirito Santo . . . . Mk. 4

SONGS AND BALLADS PUBLISHED WITHOUT OPUS NUMBER.

    I. Canzonetta (Goethe). (h.)
   II. Das Schifflein (Uhland). (h.)
 III. Das Vöglein (Holl). (m.)
 IV. Der Junggesell (Plitzer). (m.)
    V. Deutsche Flotte, Volkslied. (m.)
  VI. Die Mutter an der Wiege. (m.)
 VII. Freibeuter (Goethe). (h.)
VIII. Hinaus, hinauf, hinab! (Lasker). (h.)
  IX. In die Ferne. (h.)
    X. Nachts am Rheine. (h.)
  XI. Sängers Wanderlied (Körner).
 XII. Traumlicht. (Out of print.)
XIII. Wanderlied (Lua). (h.)
XIV. Wechsel (Goethe). (h.)
 XV. Zwist und Sühne (Simrock). Auch als Duett.

P

PART - SONGS AND OTHER WORKS.

I. Salvum fac regem, für Sop., Alt, Ten., und Bass. Partitur und
Stimmen.
II. Sechs Gesänge für vier Männerstimmen. Partitur und
Stimmen :—
    1. Das dunkle Auge (Lenau).
    2. Nachtlied (Raupach).
    3. Würde der Frauen (Schiller).
    4. Des Glockenthürmers Töchterlein (Rückert).
    5. Rüberettig (Häring).
    6. Die lustige Hochzeit.
III. Der Friede, für vier Männerstimmen (Mettlerkamp).
IV. Zwei Vaterlandslieder, für vier Männerstimmen (Hofmeis-
ter) :—
    1. Preussens Huldigung (Giesebrecht).
    2. Der deutsche Rhein (Becker).
V. Deutsche Flotte für vier Männerstimmen (Grentzensohn), auch
für eine Singstimme.
VI. Gutenberg's Bild (Giesebrecht): In dem Lichtmeer ohne
Schranke. Für Männerchor oder gemischten Chor.
VII. Zwist und Sühne (Simrock). Für zwei Singstimmen und
Pianoforte, auch für eine Singst.
VIII. "Gesänge der Stettiner Liedertafel" (Bahn). In 2 Heften :
    1. Siftungslied. 2. Otto Lied, Partitur.
IX. "Melodien des neuen Freimaurer-Gesangbuches" (Bahn). In
2 Bänden :—
    1. Auf dem ganzen Erdenrunde.
    2. Brüder, die zum Bundesfeste.
    3. Hört ihr nicht die Stimmen tönen.
    4. Wohl kennt ihr den Tempel.
    5. Schaut Brüder hin, in jene Zeiten.
    6. Welche Klagetöne schallen.
    7. Harmonie der edlen frommen Seele.
    8. Hört ein Wort aus alter Zeit.
X. Theoretische und practische Gesanglehre für Gymnasien, &c.
(Selbstverlag). (Out of print.)
XI. Klavier- und Generalbass-schule. I. und. II. Theil (Selbst-
verlag). (Out of print.)

XII. Musikalischer Gottesdienst, methodische Anweisung zum
Kirchengesange und Orgelspiel, zugleich ein vollständiges
Choralbuch (Selbstverlag). (Out of print.)
XIII. Commentar zum zweiten Theil des Goethe'schen Faust (Logier).

MANUSCRIPTS AT THE IMPERIAL LIBRARY, BERLIN. EIGHT ORATORIOS.

Palestrina. Oratorio ; the words by Giesebrecht.
Hiob. Oratorio, after the Holy Scripture, by Telschow.
Polus von Atella. Oratorio ; the words by Giesebrecht.
Der Meister von Avis. Oratorio ; the words by Giesebrecht.
Das Sühnopfer des neuen Bundes. Oratorio ; the words after the
Holy Scriptures, by Telschow.
Das hohe Lied Salomonis. Oratorio ; the words by Telschow.
Johannes der Taufer. Oratorio.
Der Segen von Assisi. Oratorio ; the words by Giesebrecht. Not
quite finished.

FOUR OPERAS.

Rudolph der deutsche Herr. Great opera ; libretto by Vocke.
Malekahdel. Great opera ; the libretto by Caroline Pichler.
Emmy. Romantic opera ; libretto by Melzer and Hauser.
Neckereien. Comic opera ; libretto by Mühlbach.
Several Cantatas, Symphonies, Concertos, Ballads, and Songs.

The right of publication of these manuscripts belongs to Frau
Julie von Bothwell, eldest daughter of Loewe.

PRINTED BY WILLIAM BLACKWOOD AND SONS.

LECTURE AND CONCERT

BALLAD AIRS OF LOEWE & SCHUBERT.

OPINIONS OF THE PRESS.

"Mr Bach essayed a bold task in giving last night a concert entirely devoted to Loewe. Had this great German composer been familiar to Edinburgh music lovers, the success of the experiment might have been less precarious. But to most amateurs, and to not a few musicians by profession, Loewe is only a name. Mr Bach, by long and careful study of Loewe's works, has become inspired with an enthusiasm for him ; and with a view to bringing the undeniably great claims of Loewe as a ballad composer prominently before us, he has chosen the bold and straightforward course of devoting an entire concert to the rendering of some of the best examples of his work........Many of his ballads are, as Mr Bach justly said in a recent lecture before the Philosophical Institution, music-dramas in miniature. If we set his 'Erlkönig' beside Schubert's, we at once recognise the different attitudes of two musicians towards the same subject. Schubert is strong in lyric beauty, Loewe in dramatic truth. Turning to last night's programme, we may say that Loewe is perhaps at his best in treating subjects with a tinge of the supernatural—as in 'The Fisher,' 'The Erl King,' 'The Night Parade,' Herr Oluf,' 'Harald,' 'Odin's Sea-ride.' These are all truly powerful examples of the highest form of ballad composition, and represent Loewe at his very best. Mr Bach, who was in capital voice, was particularly successful in these. He had entered thoroughly into the spirit of the pieces, and his vigorous and dramatic declamatory style was displayed to the best advantage, and helped to convey to the audience the true import and æsthetic value of the music........Mr Bach may be congratulated on having achieved an artistic success in this concert of Loewe's music."—*Scotsman.*

" Mr Bach's rendering of Schubert's and Loewe's ballads was a great musical treat. Schubert's setting of Goethe's ' Fischer ' and ' Erlkönig' are familiar enough, but it is seldom that they are heard to such advantage.

. . . .

" Until a few weeks ago the very name of Loewe was almost unknown here, but the lecture recently given by Mr Albert Bach to the members of the Philosophical Institution, and the admirable illustrations which accompanied it, served to introduce his compositions most effectually to the notice of all lovers of good music, and the general interest then aroused was made very evident in the support given by the public to the supplementary concert given last night........ Loewe has been fortunate in his interpreter. Mr Bach renders his ballads with all the enthusiasm of a devotee, and much of the skill and success of the highly trained artist........ His style is eminently suited to the expression of passion in all its moods, but it was a pleasure to find with what a fine contrast he was able to render the pathos and devotional significance of a more lyrical piece like ' Henry the Fowler.' "—*Leader.*

" SCHUBERT'S AND LOEWE'S BALLAD AIRS. — Under the auspices of the Edinburgh Philosophical Institution, a lecture on the above subject was delivered in the Queen Street Hall on Tuesday evening by Mr Albert B. Bach. The gifted musician had every reason to be satisfied with the reception of his lecture, and especially of his musical illustrations thereof. The lecturer emphasised the fact, that while Schubert's songs are well known, those of Loewe are rarely heard in any of our concert rooms. He claims for the latter almost an equality with Schubert as respects pure melody, and certainly the first place in point of dramatic expression. His voice was in excellent condition, and several selections from both composers were given with great power and excellent taste. The audience was large and most appreciative, and must have satisfied Mr Bach that his efforts to have justice done to a composer whom he greatly admires were not in vain."—*Glasgow Herald.*

The correspondent of the ' Cologne Gazette' writes : " Yesterday evening, an exceptionally great musical treat was given to the music lovers of Edinburgh. Mr Albert B. Bach, the much-esteemed baritone vocalist, gave a lecture on Loewe's and Schubert's ballad airs to the members of the Philosophical Institution. He illustrated the lecture in singing eight celebrated ballads of both masters. Mr Bach's main object was to introduce the hitherto here quite unknown, and even in Germany far too little cultivated, great composer Loewe. The vocalist, an ardent admirer of the great master of the ballad, was quite inspired from the dramatic character of his compositions ; and owing to Mr Bach's rich and powerful voice, and his expressive, passionate, and tasteful singing, he took the audience by storm."—*Cologne Gazette,* Monday, January 27, 1890.

WORKS BY MR ALBERT B. BACH.

WITH SOME OPINIONS OF THE PRESS.

THE PRINCIPLES OF SINGING.

A PRACTICAL GUIDE FOR VOCALISTS AND TEACHERS.

With numerous Vocal Exercises. Crown 8vo, 6s.

"As a practical guide for vocalists and teachers, Mr Bach's volume on the Principles of Singing will be found to be a thoroughly sound and lucid work. ......The work merits the highest praise that can be given, and we can heartily recommend it as a safe and practical guide to the attainment of the art of singing."—*Saturday Review.*

"The author of this work is himself a vocalist, and thus has a practical knowledge of the subject on which he writes ; he is also a musician, and he writes fluently on the science of acoustics and on the physiology of the human voice.......He deserves high commendation for the lucidity of his style in dealing with the abstruse aspects of his theme, and for the soundness of his views in that portion of his work which refers directly to voice culture.......Vocalists will find much that is interesting and helpful in the chapters on the cultivation of the voice. The directions for breathing exercises are especially good." —*Athenæum.*

"A valuable addition to the literature of Music. It is evidently the work of not only an accomplished musical artist and enthusiast, but also of one who possesses, in a high degree, the literary faculty of imparting his enthusiasm to others through the medium of written language. In the volume before us a very dry and technical subject is invested with a degree of charm that few writers on music have equalled."—*Educational Times.*

"Mr Albert Bach, whose work on 'Musical Education and Vocal Culture' may now be regarded as a classic and standard authority on the subject of which it treats, undertakes, in this volume on 'The Principles of Singing,' a more technical and practical exposition of the same subject.......The book cannot fail to impress the reader as the production of one who is at the same time an experienced teacher and an enthusiastic and accomplished artist. It deserves the attention of every student of singing."—*Scotsman.*

"A work whose value is unquestionable. It would be quite possible to write at length in praise of the work, especially of the excellent musical examples, and to commend its excellence in detail ; but the principles are set forward so clearly and agreeably, that it is not necessary to do more than heartily recommend all who are interested in the subject to buy the book and master its contents for themselves."—*Morning Post.*

"Mr Bach's book may be read with pleasure, studied with profit, and recommended with confidence.......In calling his work 'A Practical Guide,' he has not overstated its value or purpose. A perusal of the clever and genially written pages supports his assertion, and inspires the reader with a respect for the author."—*Monthly Musical Record.*

THE ART OF SINGING.

With Vocal Exercises. Crown 8vo, 3s.

"It is a most valuable addition to the aids to musical study. Written by one who is evidently a complete master of his subject, and who has earned the right to speak, the book stands almost a unique work, which, for lucidity and thoroughness, is wellnigh perfection. We will not try to enumerate a tithe of the excellences, but must confine ourselves to the more important. We know of no similar book which contains so much definite information........ The whole subject is traversed, and in a most thorough manner. Appended is a series of vocal exercises, to give opportunity for making use of directions given."—*Schoolmaster.*

"Mr Bach is so eminently practical in all he says, and invests an apparently dry subject with so much interest, that it is not easy to select particular chapters for commendation; those, however, on Vowels and Consonants, on the Equalisation of the Registers of Children's Voices, and on the Regulation of Breathing in Singing and Musical Declamation, seem to us so valuable as to call for special mention. By way of appendix there are nearly fifty pages of accompanying exercises useful in training the voice."—*School Guardian.*

ON MUSICAL EDUCATION AND VOCAL CULTURE.

Fourth Edition, Revised and Enlarged. Octavo, 7s. 6d.

"The author is a professional singer of no mean standing, and speaks with authority. The work deals chiefly with vocal rather than general musical culture, and shows not only earnestness and practicability, and an intelligent view of art, but a truly deep knowledge of the scientific branches of the question he has taken up........Signor Bach is not only scientific and literary, but he is enthusiastic as well, and a difficult and intricate subject in his hands is rendered bright and entertaining."—*Graphic.*

"Signor Bach being himself a professional singer of high standing, he is enabled to speak with authority on the subject, and his advice can be followed with confidence. He goes thoroughly and systematically into the question of the correct treatment of the voice."—*Musical Opinion.*

"The volume deals in a comprehensive and scientific manner with the production, cultivation, and preservation of the singing voice. The author is evidently not only an accomplished musician, but also a well-read physiologist, as well as a careful and painstaking teacher. Certain portions of the work cannot fail to prove of value to medical men........These we would recommend to our professional brethren as being replete with hints of great practical utility.—*Edinburgh Medical Journal.*

"His remarks upon the art of singing are extremely good, and evidently the result of much practical knowledge."—*Musical Times.*

WILLIAM BLACKWOOD & SONS, EDINBURGH AND LONDON.

www.ingramcontent.com/pod-product-compliance
Lightning Source LLC
Chambersburg PA
CBHW030326270326
41926CB00010B/1514